SECRET PALM BEACH

A Guide to the Weird, Wonderful, and Obscure

Amy Woods

Reedy Press
PO Box 5131
St. Louis, MO 63139
reedypress.com

Library of Congress Control Number: 2025948480
ISBN: 9781681066479
Design by Jill Halpin

Front cover: top left courtesy Ben Hoffman, top right courtesy Amy Woods, bottom left courtesy Palm Beach Pack & Paddle Club, bottom right courtesy Thomas Wood

Unless otherwise indicated, all photos are courtesy of the author.

Printed in the United States of America
26 27 28 29 30   5 4 3 2 1

To my parents, whose brilliant move to Palm Beach to raise a family gave me the opportunity to grow up in the Best. State. Ever.

The Casa Apava wall along the western edge of Pan's Garden

CONTENTS

Via Mizner in full bloom

ACKNOWLEDGMENTS

When I shared the news about writing *Secret Palm Beach: A Guide to the Weird, Wonderful, and Obscure*, questions came pouring in. Who is going to be in it? What is the best-kept secret? Why Palm Beach? When? Where? How?

Long before I signed a contract with Reedy Press, I spent an evening brainstorming to see whether I could actually pull off a book with such a provocative title. Armed with wine, I started scribbling weird ideas, wonderful recollections, and obscure thoughts on scraps of paper. Before I knew it, I had identified the 84 entries that appear in the pages ahead plus a few extras.

Fleshing out barely legible notes into thoughtfully composed text would not have been possible without the Gary Schweikharts and the Todd Vittums of the world. Merrell Angstreich, Tom "Buzz" Bzura, Dennis Carhart, Jim Ferguson, Jim Howe, Steve Gordon, Peter Makila, Bonnie Reuben, and many others spent their precious time with me, imparting the nuggets of knowledge I needed to build a narrative. Amanda Capote and Rose Guerrero replied to every call and every email, supplying me with a gold mine of historical facts. Mary O'Neil gave me the password to her online newspaper subscription, aiding my research.

Some of those featured in the vignettes are no longer with us, and I am grateful to their friends and relatives for openly sharing anecdotes and details, enabling me to better reveal their personalities.

To my Scotts (Benarde, Simmons, Tolley, and Velozo), I appreciate you for supporting a former coworker.

A final mention is in order for my cousin Bob, who, after realizing I had committed to the book but had not yet input a single word into the computer, reassuringly pointed to his temple and said, "It's all up here." Dude, thanks.

A perfect day on the "Wild and Scenic" Loxahatchee River

INTRODUCTION

The thrill of victory overwhelmed me when I found it. Traipsing through an ant- and iguana-populated swale in search of the last trace of a 100-year-old baseball field, I was prepared to accept the agony of defeat when, all of a sudden, the piece of history I had been hunting for came into view. As I rushed toward it, I could hear the crack of the bat, the roar of the crowd, the announcer, and the organist. I finally was standing at home plate in the exact spot where Joe DiMaggio, Mickey Mantle, and Babe Ruth took swings. I touched the weathered monument with one hand and fist-pumped with the other.

Palm Beach is full of surprises. Crown jewels and hidden gems await around every corner. Curiosities and oddities abound. From landmarked points of interest to strange-looking sculptures to a "Wild and Scenic" river, intrigue is in the air. To encounter it, you need look no further than your backyard.

By delving into *Secret Palm Beach: A Guide to the Weird, Wonderful, and Obscure*, you can experience the same frisson of excitement I did during my brush with the big leagues. You can walk down the longest hallway in the western hemisphere. You can stand on the stage where Burt Reynolds made his acting debut. If you dare, you can enter the doors of a haunted bar. Quirky things, fascinating faces, and peculiar places surround you, and as you explore the book you will discover them.

Since graduating from the University of Florida with a bachelor's degree in journalism, I have attended hundreds of pressers, interviewed thousands of sources, and written millions of words in a line of work that is all about getting to the bottom of the story. I know stuff. Let me tell you the secrets!

AWKWARD CROOK

How did the 90-degree bend on A1A get its name?

"Strolling down the avenue that's known as A1A," as Jimmy Buffett once sang, refers to the state road paralleling the Atlantic Ocean from the Florida–Georgia border to Key West. In Palm Beach, the scenic route travels past some of the poshest of pads on the island. "Mr. General Motors" lived in one of them. The head of the US automotive brand from 1923 to 1956, Alfred P. Sloan bought an estate on a section of A1A, also called South Ocean Boulevard, referred to as Billionaires Row. When the hurricane of 1947 struck, its 145-mile-per-hour winds washed five miles of infrastructure out to sea. During a massive rebuild, state officials decided to move the obliterated portion of South Ocean Boulevard closer to the Intracoastal Waterway to mitigate damage from future storm surges. In order to connect it to the unharmed portion of South Ocean Boulevard, a sharp turn was required. Sloan's Curve earned its moniker from the nearest Billionaires Row resident, who in 1990 posthumously was named one of *Life* magazine's 100 most influential Americans of the 20th century. In the years following the repairs, the county commission explored

SLOAN'S CURVE

WHAT: A haven of high-end homes attracting the world's wealthiest

WHERE: South Ocean Blvd. north of Phipps Ocean Park

COST: Free to passersby

PRO TIP: Fox News personality Sean Hannity owns two townhouses in the Residences at Sloan's Curve development.

The Alfred P. Sloan Foundation, launched in 1934 by the industrialist, helped establish the Memorial Sloan Kettering Cancer Center, a renowned research hospital in New York.

Above: *Sloan's Curve can be a danger to motorists. Photo courtesy of town of Palm Beach*

Left: *Alfred P. Sloan. Photo courtesy of Alfred P. Sloan Foundation*

the possibility of straightening the abrupt right angle—it is hazardous and associated with accidents—and ended up balking at the cost.

DAUNTING DRIVE

Why does the coquina corridor creep out all who pass through it?

Palm trees swaying above multimillion-dollar homes and meticulously trimmed hedges surrounding front yards describes most of the backdrop of the town's residential areas. Flaming bougainvillea, pastel hibiscus, and other flowering plants cheerily brighten neighborhoods when, unexpectedly, the idyllic turns into the unusual. On a strange stretch of street south of the Palm Beach Country Club, a steep rock formation appears out of nowhere and creates a cave-like effect that clashes with the otherwise pleasant greenery. Called the Coral Cut, the geological feature is the result of an infrastructure project in the 1920s that blasted through the sedimentary ridge to provide an additional road for those living on the far end of the island. North Lake Way fulfilled its purpose at a time when the population was growing in that part of town. Previously called the Coral Cliffs, portions of it reach heights of more than 20 feet and reveal a fascinating cross-section of Palm Beach's underbelly. A pump station subsequently was constructed atop the Coral Cut to facilitate the transfer of drinking water from West Palm Beach,

CORAL CUT

WHAT: 500 feet of stony spookiness

WHERE: North Lake Way

COST: Free to explore

PRO TIP: The east–west span of North Lake Way has no shoulder on either side and blind corners at both ends, so caution is advised.

In 1987, the Palm Beach Town Council designated the dramatic hardscape and some of the property near it as the Coral Cut Historic District.

The Coral Cut is the stuff of legends. Photo by Meghan McCarthy/USA Today Network via Imagn Images

and its utilitarian access point, sealed off by a metal grate, fuels the fright factor. Mechanical sounds constantly emanate from the pipe in the narrow opening, and it has come to be known by locals as the Witch's Wall.

HIDDEN HEADSTONE

Why does a primate that passed away a century ago continue to trend?

The miniature marsupial who sat on the shoulder of Palm Beach architect Addison Mizner climbed to socialite status in the 1920s. A constant companion of the man whose Mediterranean-style homes and resorts would define the look of the town, Johnnie Brown had a loyal fan club always ready with ripe bananas. Mizner owned other exotic creatures, a macaw among them, yet "the human monkey" stole the show. Johnnie Brown parlayed his popularity into a run for mayor, reportedly losing by four votes. He also received an invitation to the Scopes Trial, an important legal battle involving the prosecution of a science teacher for espousing the theory of evolution at a public school in Tennessee. So devoted was Mizner to his precious pal that he embellished a likeness of the animal on the wrought-iron gates (they are still there) leading

JOHNNIE BROWN'S GRAVE

WHAT: The final resting place of a furry friend

WHERE: Via Mizner

COST: Free to view

PRO TIP: The sepulchre stands in the courtyard of Pizza Al Fresco, enabling outdoor diners to pay their respects while digging into a tasty tomato pie.

Crotons and ferns surround Johnnie Brown's Grave.

Johnnie Brown shows his spirit on the Colony Hotel's wallpaper.

to his Worth Avenue apartment. Johnnie Brown's grave, tucked away in a plant bed on Via Mizner near the apartment, became the first burial on the island. The couple who subsequently lived in the apartment obtained permission to place their dog Laddie's grave next to Johnnie Brown's, and it became the second burial on the island. Johnnie Brown died April 30, 1927. Laddie died December 1, 1959. No other burials, for pets or people, have been allowed since.

The Colony Hotel adopted Johnnie Brown as its ambassador, giving new life to the little guy by cleverly incorporating him into the lobby's decor.

PAUPER'S FIELD

Why were hundreds of bodies forgotten about for more than six decades?

Segregation laws prevented the interment of African Americans at Woodlawn Cemetery on South Dixie Highway at the time of a destructive storm that made landfall southeast of Lake Okeechobee. The September 16 disaster caused biblical flooding and claimed as many as 3,000 lives, most of them farmworkers. Trucks hauled an approximate 1,600 bodies to a graveyard in Canal Point now known as Port Mayaca Memorial Gardens. The rest, with the exception of the hundreds burned in funeral pyres, were taken to West Palm Beach. There, a total of 674 blacks were dumped in a trench at the corner of Tamarind Avenue and 25th Street, their corpses piled on top of one another without identification. On September 30, a ceremonious hour of mourning was organized to honor the victims, and 2,000-plus sympathizers attended. The Hurricane of 1928 Mass Burial Site went unnoticed and unrecognized until 1991, when

HURRICANE OF 1928 MASS BURIAL SITE

WHAT: A desecrated ditch that turned into a sacred symbol

WHERE: 924 25th St., West Palm Beach

COST: Free to visit

PRO TIP: The protagonist in *Their Eyes Were Watching God* by Zora Neale Hurston lives in South Florida during the Hurricane of 1928 and—spoiler alert—survives.

Among the 2,000-plus sympathizers who attended the ceremonious hour of mourning after the hurricane was civil-rights activist Mary McLeod Bethune, for whom a Riviera Beach elementary school is named.

A cast-aluminum sign tells the story. Photo by Daniel Fortune

a well-publicized religious blessing took place on the grounds, prompting a local man to establish the nonprofit Storm of '28 Memorial Park Coalition. Robert Hazard pushed for the 674 blacks to receive a proper memorial, and in 2001, the trench was deemed a Florida Heritage Landmark. In 2002, it was put on the National Register of Historic Places.

CHANCERY LANE MEETS EAST ATLANTIC AVENUE

What does Jack the Ripper have to do with a local tavern?

The notorious killer from England who slashed the throats and mutilated the bodies of his victims was on a spree at the time of another murder by a jealous husband. A young woman and her lover were caught by the unassuming groom, who got rid of both of them in a fit of rage. The scene of the crime was an apartment above the Blue Anchor, a London pub where the spirit of Bertha Starkey roamed from the late 1800s until the mid-20th century. Before the pub was razed, its exterior paneling and interior features were dismantled and shipped to New York, where they were stored until 1996. That year, the Blue Anchor debuted in Delray Beach furnished with the salvaged and saved pieces from its across-the-pond namesake and its willfully attached apparition. Bertha's clamors can be heard at 10 p.m.—the

THE BLUE ANCHOR

WHAT: A bar serving plates of bangers and mash and sounds of cries and screams nightly

WHERE: 804 E Atlantic Ave., Delray Beach

COST: Happy Hour is a bargain.

PRO TIP: The Blue Anchor's signature drink is the Bloody Bertha, a transcendental take on a Bloody Mary named in honor of the eternal resident.

Two of Jack the Ripper's victims, Catherine Eddowes and Elizabeth Stride, are believed to have spent their last nights alive drinking at the original Blue Anchor.

The walls talk at the Blue Anchor. Photo by Heather Allen

time of her death—and employees used to ring the ship's bell to drown out the dreadful noise. The owner put a stop to the nightly ritual upon realizing Bertha does not like being shooed into silence. Reports of the echo of faint footsteps, the extinguishing of burning candles, and the emergence of intense warmth in various parts of the establishment continue to mount.

TOWERING TIMBER

How old is the spectacular specimen shading the Lake Trail?

Estimates put the age of the big, branched beauty at 200 years. Growing on the great lawn of the Royal Poinciana Chapel, a place of worship named after another majestic canopy, the Historic Kapok Tree amazes admirers with its buttressed trunk, horizontal crown, and, when flowering, brilliant burgundy blooms. When not staring skyward at the tree's grandeur, the enamored take pictures, record videos, and hashtag social media with selfies. The large landmark stretches some 100 feet into the air, and its snakelike roots ripple an approximate 50 feet through the grass. Situated south of the Henry Morrison Flagler Museum and north of the Society of the Four Arts, two of the town's must-see cultural institutions, the statuesque stunner is viewable via the Lake Trail. The Historic Kapok Tree is best accessed by the Royal Palm Way bridge that leads to the bicycle- and pedestrian-friendly pathway hugging the western edge of the island and overlooking the Intracoastal Waterway and downtown West Palm Beach. Members of the chapel's administration and staff proudly (and strictly) steward the tree and the rest of the cloistered grounds that include the Olivia and Walter Kiebach Memorial Garden and the Dudley Moore Family Fountain, which both honor late parishioners. Together, the lushly landscaped environs provide an area for peaceful reflection and quiet contemplation.

Due to unfortunate defacement, a fence was installed to prevent visitors from climbing across the tree's trunk and carving their names in its bark.

HISTORIC KAPOK TREE

WHAT: An awe-inspiring, arboreal attraction

WHERE: 315 Chapel Hill Rd.

COST: Free to view

PRO TIP: The Historic Kapok Tree has its own Tripadvisor page, and at last count it had 45 reviews.

The Historic Kapok Tree has stood sentinel for two centuries.

FINDER'S FOLLY

What can be had inside the treasure trove?

Labels, and lots of them. The 4,500-square-foot resale store collects clothing—think top-of-the-line designer couture—and accessories such as swanky handbags, expensive jewelry, and gorgeous watches. All of it comes from wealthy Palm Beachers who either tired of their possessions, moved out of their homes, or are dearly departed. Rare books and fine china fill much of the merchandise-stuffed shelves. One shopper smiled upon seeing a copy of the *Glory of Woman*, a hardcover authored in 1896 by Drs. Monfort B. Allen and Amelia C. McGregor that imparts universal, although outdated, advice and information on love and marriage. Another shopper speedily snapped up a set of gadroon-shaped, hand-painted Spode Thanksgiving plates that date to the early 20th century. Crystal pieces arrive at the store frequently, along with electronics, kitchenware, and

THE CHURCH MOUSE

WHAT: An elevated thrift shop that benefits charity

WHERE: 376 S County Rd.

COST: Expect to pay more than at a Goodwill store.

PRO TIP: Hours are 10 a.m. to 5 p.m. Mondays through Saturdays from August to June.

Left: *Outerwear crowds a corner of the Church Mouse. Photo by Rachel Sanelli*

Opposite: *A symmetrical brick facade is a distinguishing element of the Church Mouse's exterior. Photo by Marisa Holliday*

shoes. Artwork, furniture, lamps, pillows, and other items get picked up, priced, and purchased on a day-to-day basis. Operated by volunteers, the store funnels all proceeds to outreach programs at the Church of Bethesda-by-the-Sea that focus on education, food, shelter, and basic human needs. The town council deemed the Church Mouse a landmark in accordance with a historic-preservation ordinance that protects significant sites on the island. The building, designed in 1936 by John Volk, exemplifies the renowned architect's Georgian Revival style.

John Volk studied architecture at New York's Columbia University and landed in Palm Beach in the mid-1920s with a client list that included the Pulitzers and the Vanderbilts.

SYMBOLIC SHRINE

Why do the stained-glass windows of the sanctuary radiate onto the street?

The vibrant *ventanas* in St. Mark's Episcopal Church's Peace Chapel take viewers to a place of calm and comfort—the water. Four of the color-drenched windows frame a chiseled stone altar. Two larger ones, at six feet wide by 14 feet tall, jut out from the building at 45-degree angles and catch light from the rising and setting sun. The city of Palm Beach Gardens approved the ornate openings, masterfully handblown by a Florida crafter, as an official Art in Public Places project. Visible to motorists, the vignettes depict a pelican and several ospreys in flight, a green sea turtle and tropical reef fish swimming below, and aquatic flora emerging from the bottom. More stained glass covers the east and west walls as well as the double doors at the entrance. The chapel is open to the public 24/7 for mediation, prayer, soul-searching, or simply to bask in its glow. At noon every Friday, gatherers recite the Litany of Forgiveness, an incantation that originated

Above: *A pair of bottle palms adds to the ambiance of the Peace Chapel.*

Opposite: *Warm-water whimsy fills every pane.*

at Coventry Cathedral in England in response to its bombing during World War II. St. Mark's Episcopal Church is one of hundreds of Coventry Cathedral partners worldwide that belong to the Community Cross of Nails, an international movement seeking global tolerance and understanding.

PEACE CHAPEL

WHAT: A petite nave with South Florida flair

WHERE: 3395 Burns Rd., Palm Beach Gardens

COST: Free to visit

PRO TIP: A section of flooring in the Peace Chapel is patterned like an old labyrinth, a circular, enclosed pathway to be walked in spiritual tradition.

Palm Beach Gardens's Art in Public Places program makes sure aesthetics thrive amid development by requiring builders, per city ordinance, to fund installations.

BROTHERHOOD OF BIKERS

Where does the pack of black-and-red-wearing riders rally?

A chain-link fence and a metal gate front a dark-gray building on the edge of a Riviera Beach residential area. A lit sign with sinister lettering on the facade reads, "Enforcers Motorcycle Club Mother Chapter." Here, members of the trademarked national organization hold court. The Mother Chapter is headquarters for the 46 clubs in 12 states and one club in Canada that have banded together to enjoy America's freedoms. Those who have earned their patch-covered vests come from careers in law enforcement, the military, and public safety and share an interest in meeting others to celebrate motorcycle culture. Established in 2000 by Rick "Rosco" Sessa, the club puts on monthly First Friday concerts, organizes a national conference each January, and supports charities including Special Olympics and Wreaths Across America plus local bicycle giveaways and holiday toy drives.

The Enforcers Motorcycle Club Mother Chapter is a 501(c)7 nonprofit.

The "5665" on the shrouded silver sword in the club's medieval-looking logo translates, numerically to alphabetically, to "Enforcers Forever, Forever Enforcers."

ENFORCERS MOTORCYCLE CLUB MOTHER CHAPTER

WHAT: An organization of two-wheeling enthusiasts who love their leather

WHERE: 1525 Ave. E, Riviera Beach

COST: Donations are optional.

PRO TIP: To frequent the First Friday concerts or any other club happenings, one has to be a friend of a member.

Members park their preferred method of transportation in front of the club.

Sessa, a retired police lieutenant commander with 21 years on the force, serves as national president. He began riding a Honda dirt bike at age 8 and now owns four Harley-Davidsons, one Indian, and his grandfather's 1971 Moto Guzzi. His teenage dream was to belong to a motorcycle club. The black and red colors represent the mourning of fallen officers and the blood lost in battle.

FEARLESS FARMERS

Who is Sukeji Morikami, and more importantly, who is Jo Sakai?

The two immigrants from Miyazu, a city in the Kyoto region of Japan, settled halfway around the world in northern Boca Raton to colonize and plant crops. The year was 1906. Jo Sakai ambitiously recruited other young men, including Sukeji Morikami, promising them abundance through agriculture with the harvesting of winter vegetables. Their village, called Yamato after Japan's ancient name, thrived for a short period until yields started to fall. It ultimately became unsustainable. While the American dream did not turn into reality for the two dozen families who toiled in the dirt, some stayed and started families. Sakai's wife, Sada, was the first woman in Yamato, and she gave birth to its first baby. Sadly, Hiroshi, their son, died before age 2. Sakai died in 1923 at age 49. Morikami, the last of the original colonists, managed to buy back some of the property confiscated by the US government for use as a military base during World War II, property that would become the Morikami Museum and Japanese

MORIKAMI MUSEUM AND JAPANESE GARDENS

WHAT: A living monument to the Asian American experience

WHERE: 4000 Morikami Park Rd., Delray Beach

COST: Fee for admission

PRO TIP: Hours are 10 a.m. to 5 p.m. Tuesdays through Sundays, with the café serving Asian cuisine from 11 a.m. to 3 p.m.

Sukeji Morikami died in 1976 at age 91 with no heirs, and had it not been for "George's" philanthropic gift, the Yamato legacy likely would have been lost.

Left: *Sukeji Morikami*

Right: *Jo Sakai*

Above: *Cascading waterfalls are one of the features of the Morikami Museum and Japanese Gardens that portray the natural wonder of Japan. Photos courtesy of Morikami Museum and Japanese Gardens*

Gardens. He successfully reaped and sowed it, finally finding the abundance through agriculture promised to him so many years ago. In 1973, the reclusive man known as "George" donated nearly 200 acres to Palm Beach County in the interest of preserving the history of Yamato.

FIELDS OF DREAMS

Who is the National Baseball Hall of Famer cheering on the athletes?

Considered the greatest catcher of all time, Johnny Bench retired from professional sports in 1983. The former Cincinnati Red enshrined at the museum in Cooperstown, New York, now lives the good life in the Sunshine State, where he is leaving a legacy that will last as long as his franchise-record homers and RBIs. Bench, the National League Rookie of the Year in 1968 and MVP in 1970 and 1972 who won back-to-back World Series titles in 1975 and 1976, supports the Miracle League of Palm Beach County. He devotes his time and his talent to the 250 youths served by the organization and stands behind its mission of making sure every child has the opportunity to play ball. He also attends the nonprofit's Dinner on the Diamond benefit every year. The league comprises 10 teams named after the pastime's favorites—Astros, Cardinals, Marlins, Nationals, Rays, and Yankees—plus a cheerleading crew. The action

THE MIRACLE LEAGUE OF PALM BEACH COUNTY

WHAT: A squad of special-needs children overcoming their disabilities

WHERE: 4029 Johnson Dairy Rd., Palm Beach Gardens, and 1905 SW Fourth Ave., Delray Beach

COST: Free to play

PRO TIP: Donations to the Miracle League of Palm Beach County can be made by calling 561-414-4441 or by visiting miracleleaguepalmbeachcounty.com.

The Dinner on the Diamond benefit, a tented to-do atop the artificially turfed play area, raises funds to ensure a no-fee future for the league.

Johnny Bench and his wife, Carmen, pose with Julia Kadel (left), cofounder and executive director of the Miracle League of Palm Beach County. Photo courtesy of MasterWing Creative Agency

unfolds on no-obstacle, wheelchair-friendly fields in Palm Beach Gardens and Delray Beach. One of 14 leagues in Florida and 350 in the United States, Australia, Canada, Mexico, New Zealand, and Puerto Rico, its season runs from the end of March to the end of May and culminates with the smile-inducing All-Star games.

HOT PROPERTY

Where did the death-obsessed Doors singer live the first six months of his life?

Way before he met Pam, his common-law wife and the inspiration for the hit "Love Street," Jim Morrison spent his infancy in Melbourne, a city four counties north of Palm Beach. He was born December 8, 1943, in Brevard Hospital, now Holmes Regional Medical Center, to parents George and Clara Morrison. The Florida native who would achieve sex-symbol status crawled around in a small, single-family bungalow and frolicked on the beach nearby. His father, a Naval Academy graduate, was flight training at Naval Air Station Melbourne in preparation for deployment in the Pacific Theater. When the pilot shipped out in the Spring of 1944, Clara Morrison took their infant son to Clearwater and stayed with her in-laws. A daring, erratic, and frequently unpredictable binge drinker, the photogenic phenom died in 1971 at age 27. The privately owned home went on the market in 2022 for a whopping $2.5 million. The local Realtor (and music junkie) who had the listing stood by its presumptuous price. The digits dropped to $2.4 million and then

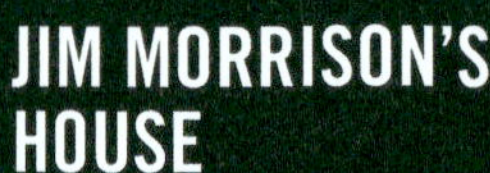

JIM MORRISON'S HOUSE

WHAT: 1,856 square feet of rock-'n'-roll history

WHERE: 2100 Vernon Pl., Melbourne

COST: Not for sale

PRO TIP: A recent appraisal valued the modest abode at $315,500.

Above: *The modest abode is one block south of Melbourne's main drag and one block north of Crane Creek.*

Opposite: *Jim Morrison attended Florida State University in Tallahassee before transferring to the University of California, Los Angeles. Photos by Elaine New*

to $1.9 million, and by the end of the year, the listing had been removed. It sports a red-and-white paint job, has photos and sketches of the '60s idol in the front windows, and occasionally attracts in-the-know fans.

Brevard County records show the wood-frame, stucco structure sold for $38,900 in 1978, $40,000 in 1989, $135,000 in 2006, and $225,000 in 2007.

DREAMY DIGS

How did the late Beatle come to own an oceanfront estate on the island?

The period in John Lennon's life referred to as the "Lost Weekend" brought him to Florida and, specifically, to the Sun and Surf condominiums. In 1974, he stayed at the complex on Sunrise Avenue with son Julian and love interest May Pang during a separation from wife Yoko Ono. According to a news report, Lennon said he adored Palm Beach and wanted to invest in a piece of property in the area. Long after their 18-month marital split was over, Lennon and Ono purchased a $725,000 Addison Mizner–designed masterpiece in January of 1980. They decided to renovate it for use as a vacation home. Plans never got that far. On December 8 of that year, Lennon was murdered. Ono eventually had the house restored and sold it for $3.1 million in February of 1986. The 13,730-square-foot Mediterranean-style dwelling called El Solano has sheltered its share of celebrities throughout the decades. Socialite Brownie McLean—married to John McLean, the Hope Diamond heir—lived there until she sold it to Lennon and Ono. During that

JOHN LENNON'S HOUSE

WHAT: A mansion that once belonged to the peace-crusading member of the Fab Four

WHERE: 720 S Ocean Blvd.

COST: Not for sale

PRO TIP: A recent appraisal valued El Solano at $32.3 million.

El Solano is named for the California county near the North Bay region of San Francisco where Addison Mizner was born and raised.

Above: *El Solano has 180 feet of ocean frontage. Photo courtesy of Preservation Foundation of Palm Beach Archives*

Left: *John Lennon and Yoko Ono were photographed by the* New York Times *on November 2, 1980, in what turned out to be an historic session. Photo by Jack Mitchell*

time, naughty-magazine publisher Larry Flynt rented the place—he used a fake name to get away with it—and photographed nude models on-site. New residents paid $23 million for El Solano in 2016, and in 2020, they sold it for $36 million.

WOODSTOCK SOUTH

What really happened during the weekend concert in 1969?

It rained relentlessly. Temperatures plummeted into the low 40s. Fans waited for the final act of the Palm Beach International Music and Arts Festival, the Rolling Stones, who took the stage more than 10 hours late, and impatiently started rogue fires to keep warm. As dusk turned to dawn, Mick Jagger uttered the last note, Keith Richards struck the last chord, and Charlie Watts hit the last beat of a set that fell flat. At one point, Jagger mistakenly gave a shout-out to Miami, a world away from the motorsports park in rural Palm Beach County where 50,000 free spirits dazedly shared their '60s-ism. The multiday event saw performances from, among others, Iron Butterfly, King Crimson, Johnny Winter, and Janis Joplin. Joplin brandished a bottle of her beverage of choice, Southern Comfort, during her appearance and was said to have skinny-dipped at the Colonnades Beach Hotel, festival headquarters, afterward. Sweetwater, the band that opened Woodstock three months earlier, also played as did Sly and the Family Stone, the Byrds, Grand Funk Railroad, Steppenwolf, and Jefferson Airplane. In 2012, the Palm Beach International Raceway commemorated the festival's 43rd anniversary with the unveiling of a historical marker at a ceremony attended by Mark Stein, the original keyboardist for Vanilla Fudge, which was on the bill, too.

Both the Rolling Stones and the Byrds declined invitations to Woodstock, the original three-days-of-peace-and-music blowout that unfolded on a muddy dairy farm in New York and shape-shifted popular culture.

Top: *Toting blankets and sleeping bags, the faithful flock to the Palm Beach International Music and Arts Festival.*

Bottom: *Mark Stein, of Vanilla Fudge, remembers the Palm Beach International Music and Arts Festival. Photos by Ken Davidoff*

PALM BEACH INTERNATIONAL MUSIC AND ARTS FESTIVAL

WHAT: A star-studded jam session

WHERE: 17047 Beeline Hwy., Jupiter

COST: $20

PRO TIP: The Palm Beach International Raceway closed in 2022 after the owners decided to sell the two-and-a-quarter-mile circuit and the rest of its 150 acres to developers.

FLOATING RELIC

How did a pristine presidential yacht that nearly sank make way?

The 93-footer whose cabins accommodated five commanders in chief, most notably John F. Kennedy, piqued the interest of a local developer with a penchant for high-end watercrafts. Charlie Modica did not hesitate to invest in a $20 million restoration project to save the vessel and preserve its history. *Honey Fitz* belonged to President Kennedy from 1961 to 1963. The part-time Palm Beacher named it in honor of his maternal grandfather John Francis "Honey Fitz" Fitzgerald. First lady Jacqueline Kennedy edited the interior to meet her flawless taste. Even though Presidents Harry S Truman, Dwight D. Eisenhower, Lyndon

HONEY FITZ

WHAT: An icon adorned with the seal of the highest office in the land

WHERE: 1065 N A1A, Jupiter

COST: Call 561-693-5063 for charter inquiries.

PRO TIP: *Honey Fitz*, whose new home on the Loxahatchee River faces the Jupiter Inlet Lighthouse, can be admired and photographed from the water.

Left: *Old Glory flutters behind the sun deck.*

Below: Honey Fitz *looks timeless at 95-plus years of age. Photos by Carmel Brantley*

B. Johnson, and Richard M. Nixon also laid claim to the perk of the job, its refurbishment reflects the John and Jackie era. Constructed in 1931 for Sewell Avery, the chairman of Montgomery Ward, it was requisitioned by the US government in 1942 for military use. In 1971, it was purchased at an auction after being decommissioned by President Nixon and had a subsequent owner before it was found deteriorating in a South Florida canal. *Honey Fitz* spent the next three years in the yard and is shipshape once more with a new purpose as a charter. Parties of up to 35 can enjoy a jaunt on the Intracoastal Waterway with a nod to the famous family.

The effort to return *Honey Fitz* to its 1960s-era stateliness entailed reproducing the cushioned furniture, including President Kennedy's big blue chair on the aft deck.

WILDMAN OF THE LOXAHATCHEE

Who shot Vincent Natulkiewicz?

Little evidence and lots of speculation about the strapping survivalist found five days after a single shotgun wound to the chest killed him still circulate. One thing historians agree on is that while somebody knows the answer, the public probably never will. The story begins in 1931, when a young drifter from New Jersey hopped on a train bound for Florida and hopped off when he saw Jupiter. Vince Nelson, the shortened version of his Polish name, liked the sparsity of the small farming community along the Loxahatchee River. He trapped animals to make a living, leading to the title by which he was widely known. At first a hometown curiosity, Trapper Nelson and his cobbled-together camp quickly morphed into a tourist attraction. The *Tarzan* movies had reached their peak that decade, and the six-foot, two-inch, 200-pound hunk

TRAPPER NELSON

WHAT: The restored homestead of a legendary character who made his home on the brush-filled riverbank

WHERE: Jonathan Dickinson State Park, Hobe Sound

COST: Fee for admission and the boat tour (see below)

PRO TIP: The Trapper Nelson Interpretive Site can be accessed on the boat tour or by paddling to the grounds.

Although no suspects and no charges emerged in Trapper Nelson's death, fingers still point, theories still float, and the question of whether it was suicide still looms.

Above: *Trapper Nelson, with a snake around his neck and a fur around his waist, awaits guests at his camp. Photo courtesy of Loxahatchee River Historical Society*

Left: *Trapper Nelson rarely wore a shirt and liked to play up his Tarzan image. Photo by Richard Little*

seemed like the living embodiment of the character. Nelson readily took to his popularity and staged live shows with alligators and snakes. He built cabins to accommodate overnight guests. In 1960, his run on the river came to an end when he closed his camp. Now a recluse in his 50s, he was dealing with health problems at a time when greedy developers in a fast-growing Jupiter wanted to grab his land. A friend found him face down in the dirt.

FOOTBALL FACTORY

Where did a multitude of NFL players hone their skills?

Lawrence Chester, a cornerback for the Atlanta Falcons and the Detroit Lions, attended Lake Shore High School in Belle Glade. When he was drafted in 1967, he became the first varsity footballer from the rural Lake Okeechobee region to play with the big boys. Since then, dozens of talented teenagers have gone from being in the muck to being in the money. Rickey Jackson, drafted in 1981 by the New Orleans Saints, was enshrined in the Pro Football Hall of Fame in 2010. Anquan Boldin, drafted in 2003 by the Arizona Cardinals, earned the Walter Payton NFL Man of the Year Award in 2015. Both Pahokee Middle-Senior High School graduates are recognized in the Hall of Honor at the Lawrence E. Will Museum of the Glades, where their photos, highlights, and backgrounds bedeck the walls. They are joined by Santonio Holmes, a standout athlete for Glades Central Community High School who was named Super Bowl XLIII MVP after his game-winning, foot-dragging touchdown catch for the Pittsburgh Steelers in their

LAWRENCE E. WILL MUSEUM OF THE GLADES

WHAT: A salute to homegrown heroes of the gridiron

WHERE: 530 S Main St., Belle Glade

COST: Admission is free.

PRO TIP: The Lawrence E. Will Museum of the Glades is open from 10 a.m. to 3 p.m. Mondays through Thursdays.

The Glades has another vital industry on which it relies—farming—and its fertile soil known as "black gold" yields celery, green beans, radishes, sweet corn, and sugar cane.

The Hall of Honor looks back on the role of the Glades and its impact on the contact sport. Photo by Cheryl Stein

27–23 defeat of the Arizona Cardinals. Other Glades Central Community High School graduates deservedly given space in the exhibit include first-round draft picks Jessie Hester, Louis Oliver, and Fred Taylor. In all, more than 70 locally bred NFL players are recognized in the display.

COTTON CLUB OF THE SOUTH

Who gigged at the downtown juke joint during the Big Band era?

Louis Armstrong, Count Basie, James Brown, Cab Calloway, Duke Ellington, and Ella Fitzgerald ruled the Big Band era of American music, and each one let it rip at the swinging venue that opened in the early 1920s as the Sunset Roof Garden and Grill. "Satchmo" sounded his trumpet, Basie pounded his piano, and the "Godfather of Soul" strutted his stuff. Calloway scatted, Ellington led his orchestra, and the "First Lady of Song" hit the high—and low—notes. Now known as the Sunset Lounge, the vaunted establishment changed names several times. The Sunset Roof Garden and Grill became the Sunset Royale Night Club, and after an expansion to include a first-floor bar, a second-floor ballroom, and an elevated stage, it became the Sunset Auditorium. In the late 1940s, the owner sold the business,

SUNSET LOUNGE

WHAT: An extensively overhauled building where African American culture abounded

WHERE: 609 Eighth St., West Palm Beach

COST: To be determined when open

PRO TIP: The city is in the process of sending out solicitations to find an operator for the former nexus of black society.

When it was called the Sunset Auditorium, the venue was a booming dance hall and was featured in the *Crisis*, the official publication of the NAACP.

The Sunset Lounge marquee brightens the street corner once more.

and it was rebranded again as the Sunset Cocktail Lounge. In 1977, the second-floor ballroom was converted into apartments, and up until 2018, the first-floor bar was open for business. The West Palm Beach Community Redevelopment Agency came to the rescue of the run-down building in 2022 and sank $16 million into a multiyear project to bring back the face of the Historic Northwest District. When completed, the Sunset Lounge will reinvigorate the neighborhood and serve as a cultural destination.

NOTEWORTHY GROUNDS

What does the eclectic open space symbolize?

Paved trails curving around neat landscaping take visitors on an animated journey through the lives of famous musicians of color. Depictions of a smiling Ike and Tina Turner and a smirking Fats Waller are showcased on mosaic benches. Ray Charles appears in his signature shades on a seat wall. Cole looks as cool as he sounds farther down the way. A pair of columns bears the names of Louis Armstrong and Ella Fitzgerald. A tribute to the powerhouse players of the 20th century, Heart & Soul Park represents the sounds that emanated from the adjacent Sunset Lounge, where many of them performed. The park features a set of chimes, a xylophone, and other interactive instruments set up amid slides and swings protected by shade sails. A statement-making copper sculpture created by Washington, DC, artist Nekisha Durrett punctuates the scenery. *Genius Loci* (it means pervading spirit) is a colossal gramophone that imaginatively funnels voices from the past, and not solely those of singers. The piece prompts viewers to hear the stories

HEART & SOUL PARK

WHAT: An outdoor homage to the Historic Northwest District's black roots

WHERE: 825 N Rosemary Ave., West Palm Beach

COST: Free to explore

PRO TIP: On the same street less than one mile south is Publix, a favorite grocery store where a drink and a snack can be picked up to enjoy at the park.

Heart & Soul Park is part of the Palm Beach County Black Cultural Heritage Trail, a self-guided tour with points of interest that honor the African American experience.

Genius Loci *glows in the afternoon sun.*

of those who lived in the Styx, a community of poor laborers building hotels for Henry Morrison Flagler. In 1894, a suspicious fire destroyed their homes, referenced by chunks of charred wood surrounding the gramophone's pedestal.

ONCE A BARRIER, NOW A BRIDGE

Why is the structure that represented segregation still standing?

Healthier Lake Worth Beach, a resident-driven initiative to better blighted pockets of the community, identified the 1,200-foot-long, six-foot-tall strip of concrete as an improvement project. The divider was erected in 1954 to confine families living in an area annexed as the Osborne Colored Addition and keep them out of Whispering Palms, a section of white-owned homes across the street. The Osborne Colored Addition was the lone part of the city where African American

---

Whispering Palms formed a neighborhood association that is creating a book about the transformation of the Lake Worth Beach Unity Wall and recognizing families from the Osborne Colored Addition.

The power of expression is evident on the Lake Worth Beach Unity Wall. Photo by Daniel Fortune

households were permitted in accordance with Jim Crow laws. In 2021, forward-thinking citizens on both sides of the pale agreed an action plan was necessary to right past wrongs. They decided that instead of tearing it down, they would beautify it and give it a name. Volunteers cleaned it, repaired it, and painted it. Murals of national black icons and local black politicians cover the Lake Worth Beach Unity Wall along with scenes of hand-holding and hearts. Inspirational phrases and quotes are interspersed throughout. Diversity is a key theme in the illustrations by amateur artists who donated their time and professional artists who donated their talent. Funding from the Palm Health Foundation and other partners ensures the wall is properly maintained in an ongoing effort to change the narrative of the stigmatic symbol.

LAKE WORTH BEACH UNITY WALL

WHAT: A repurposed remnant of black history

WHERE: 1426 Wingfield St.

COST: Free to explore

PRO TIP: Retha Lowe, represented on the Lake Worth Beach Unity Wall, was the city's first black commissioner and later became vice mayor.

SECLUDED BEAUTY

What lies in wait at the end of eight intriguing easements?

The fountains, murals, sculptures, and other surprises along a series of decorative walkways off Palm Beach's main drag can turn a window-shopping stroll into an all-afternoon adventure. Subtle charm fills Via Amore, Via Bice, Via Encantada, Via Mario, Via Mizner, Via Newsome, Via Parigi, and Via Roma. Clothing boutiques and jewelry stores are in the mix as are antiques dealers, art galleries, and restaurants. A fair share of interior-design firms and real-estate agencies also occupy the elegant spaces. What makes Worth Avenue's vias so enchanting, though, are their arched entries and Mexican tile, their colorful flowers and manicured foliage, and their mysterious doors that lead to who knows where. At the end of Via Amore, a collection of brightly painted bronzes by Monyo Mihailescu-Nasturel (he is a descendant of a Romanian king and is a longtime Palm Beach resident known as Prince Monyo) depict children in various states of play. At the end

WORTH AVENUE'S VIAS

WHAT: Resplendent pedestrian paths often overlooked

WHERE: Worth Ave.

COST: Tickets for the walking tour can be purchased in advance.

PRO TIP: No trip to Worth Avenue is complete without venturing across South Ocean Boulevard to the stately coquina clock tower for a photo.

During season, the Worth Avenue Association's historical docent leads groups up and down the spotless sidewalks during an anecdote-filled morning of architectural and historical highlights.

Above: *Love is in the air on Via Amore.*

Left: *Via Roma is the narrowest of the eight.*

of Via Mizner, Italian dining stronghold Renato's Palm Beach whips up its hallowed handmade ravioli. At the end of Via Roma, a literary-themed coffee shop invites customers to sip a Murder on the Orient Espresso or a To Kill a Macchiato. While Worth Avenue, at three blocks, is relatively short, its delightful detours can take most of the day to explore.

GRANDE DAME

How did the cereal heiress end up living on South Ocean Boulevard?

Mar-a-Lago, the exquisite estate whose Spanish name means sea to lake, rose from 17 acres of overgrown terrain that the wife of well-known stockbroker E.F. Hutton chose as the location for a home like no other. École des Beaux-Arts–educated architect Marion Sims Wyeth designed the courtyard-centric floor plan. Marjorie Merriweather Post, the owner of the Postum company following the 1914 suicide of her 59-year-old father Charles William "C.W." Post, tasked architect Joseph Urban with the wow factor. Urban, a friend of Florenz Ziegfeld and the creator of the flamboyant producer's original theater at 54th Street and Sixth Avenue in New York, added archways, frescoes, tiles, and a wondrous ballroom to the 115-room layout, crowning it with an ornamental Moorish tower. Mar-a-Lago was completed in 1927. The fabulously wealthy couple continued to winter at their island palace until their divorce in 1935. By that time, the 48-year-old had three daughters by two husbands and would marry twice more. She spent the remainder of her life as a

Marjorie Merriweather Post. Photo courtesy of Hillwood Estate, Museum & Gardens, Archives and Special Collections

Mar-a-Lago bares its unmistakable profile. Photo by Jud McCranie

philanthropist supporting major causes and welcoming dignitaries onto her magnificent property for fundraisers. In 1944, she opened an occupational-therapy program on the grounds for injured World War II soldiers. She died in 1973 at age 86. In 1981, her foundation put Mar-a-Lago up for sale. Donald Trump bought it in 1985.

MARJORIE MERRIWEATHER POST

WHAT: The former address of a privileged pacesetter whose vast riches shaped the annals of the island

WHERE: 1100 S Ocean Blvd.

COST: Private club

PRO TIP: When President Trump is in town, the Palm Beach County Sheriff's Office and the Secret Service set up checkpoints at the Southern Boulevard traffic circle.

Movie star Dina Merrill, Marjorie Merriweather Post's oldest daughter who died in 2017 at age 93, spent many a season at Mar-a-Lago and slept in the quaint children's suite.

ART HISTORY

Where did Salvador Dalí paint the oil on canvas?

The Spanish nobleman and the Spanish surrealist met in Paris. The bon vivants ran in similar circles, George de Cuevas with his zeal for dance and Salvador Dalí with his zest for art. They became friends in the years leading up to World War II and in 1940, fled France for the United States to escape the German invasion. Cuevas lived in a 12,700-square-foot home on Palm Beach's El Bravo Way and invited Dalí to stay at the estate for extended periods of time. In 1942, while a houseguest, Dalí created the 24-by-32-inch work that depicts the marquis, stern and suited, standing before a saturnine landscape that includes a windblown cypress tree and a hunched-over male figure. The cypress tree represents the inevitability of death and features an intriguing circular staircase winding up to a darkened doorway nestled among the branches. The male figure is a reference to Jean-Hippolyte Flandrin's *Study (Young Male Nude Seated Beside the Sea)* and hints at homosexuality. Cuevas was married to Margaret Rockefeller Strong, a

PORTRAIT OF MARQUIS GEORGE DE CUEVAS

WHAT: A framed masterpiece that came to life at a Palm Beach address

WHERE: 343 El Bravo Way

COST: Not for sale

PRO TIP: Lithographs of other works by Salvador Dalí are available for acquisition at Onessimo Fine Art in Palm Beach Gardens.

Portrait of Marquis George de Cuevas debuted at the Norton Museum of Art in 2013 as a Masterpiece of the Month and has remained on loan since.

Above: *Palm Beach placed 343 El Bravo Way on the list of town landmarks in 1989.*

Left: Portrait of Marquis George de Cuevas *is rife with symbolism. Photo courtesy of Fundació Gala-Salvador Dalí, Artists Rights Society*

granddaughter of John D. Rockefeller, fathered two children with her, and made her a widow when he died in 1961 at age 75, yet it was common knowledge the ballet impresario was gay.

TALK OF THE TOWN

What famed firm is responsible for the original design of Lake Park?

The urban-planning company founded in 1865 by Frederick Law Olmsted—the pioneer of American landscape architecture whose impressive portfolio includes Central Park in New York, Jackson Park in Chicago, and Grant Park in Atlanta as well as the Biltmore Estate in Asheville, North Carolina—plotted the 2.4-square-mile municipality. The year was 1919, and by that time Olmsted's sons had taken over the business. Harry Seymour Kelsey, a Boston transplant who bought and developed the land, hired the Olmsted Brothers to come up with the schematic. The Olmsted Brothers carved the area into three distinct districts that appear much like they did a century ago. The residential blocks to the east and the industrial blocks to the west border the commercial blocks in the middle. The most Olmsted-esque feature of the town is Kelsey Park and its pavilion-dotted green spaces, meandering walkways, and bubbling fountain. Incorporated in 1923 as Kelsey City, it was advertised as "the world's winter playground" and flaunted a showy archway to welcome prospective homeowners. In 1939, the town changed its name to

Above: *The archway leading to Kelsey Park is an homage to the archway that led to Kelsey City.*

Opposite: *Flags fly in front of Lake Park Town Hall.*

Lake Park. The building at 918 Park Avenue is an original structure, and an approximate 100 others, most of them in the residential blocks, are original, too. Lake Park Town Hall at 535 Park Avenue is listed on the National Register of Historic Places.

PEDIGREED PLATS

WHAT: A notable neighborhood mapped out by creators of landmarks

WHERE: Lake Park

COST: Free to explore

PRO TIP: The town's much-loved Sunset Celebration brings arts, crafts, and food vendors plus live music to Kelsey Park the last Friday of the month.

The architectural styles of Lake Park's first houses range from Craftsman Bungalow to Spanish Eclectic, and many of those that remain standing are marked with historic plaques.

STORIED SEAFARER

What criminal mastermind owned the prized craft?

Bernie Madoff died in 2021 at age 82 while serving a 150-year prison sentence for defrauding investors out of $65 billion. The convicted Ponzi-schemer's five-bedroom, seven-bathroom Palm Beach estate was seized in 2009 by the US Marshals Service along with an amassed personal fortune that included three boats. One of them was a 1969 Rybovich. Designed for a descendant of a local pioneer family, the 56-footer was special from the start. Expert builder Tommy Rybovich sculpted 79 hulls during his career and considered the 71st, to be named *Apava*, his favorite. Madoff acquired *Apava* in 1979 and tempted fate by changing its name to *Bull*. He and Ruth Madoff used it as a pleasure cruiser and frequently were seen

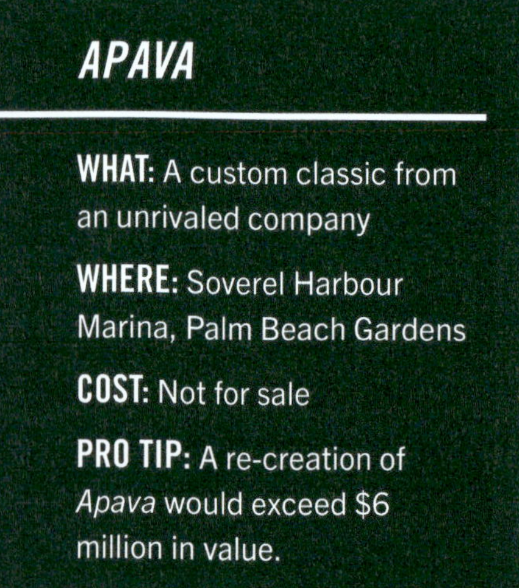

APAVA

WHAT: A custom classic from an unrivaled company

WHERE: Soverel Harbour Marina, Palm Beach Gardens

COST: Not for sale

PRO TIP: A re-creation of *Apava* would exceed $6 million in value.

The air-conditioned interior of Apava *has all the comforts of home.*

Apava's teak deck gleams.

out and about on the Intracoastal Waterway. *Bull* eventually was purchased at an asset-forfeiture auction and, after changing hands several times, ended up in the loving arms of three brothers-in-law with a passion for vintage vessels. They shepherded the old gal to a local marina and willingly and ably sunk money into it. Following four months of repairs, the sport fisher with the double handrail and a broken sheer—Rybovich signatures—had returned to glory. *Apava* now makes waves in South Florida, the Bahamas, and the Chesapeake Bay.

Apava (it is Hindu for "he who sports in the water") got its moniker from the Casa Apava estate where the original owner grew up.

CACOPHONY OF COLORS

How did the clothing line and its splashy hues get started?

Necessity is the mother of invention, and when an adventurous socialite faced a Cadillac problem, she stumbled upon a brilliant solution. The young wife of Herbert Pulitzer, the citrus grove–owning grandson of prominent publisher Joseph Pulitzer, for whom the Pulitzer Prize is named, decided to fill her spare time by selling fresh-squeezed juice at an outdoor stand on Worth Avenue. She constantly was spilling the pulpy liquid of grapefruits and oranges onto her outfits and wanted to create a polychromatic uniform that would camouflage stains. A simple cotton silhouette stitched together by her seamstress would give rise to the classic shift. Customers immediately noticed her new wardrobe and said they loved the combinations of greens, pinks, sky blues, and sunny yellows. She had her seamstress make more and offered them for sale. Palm Beachers snapped

LILLY PULITZER

WHAT: The birth of American resort wear

WHERE: Boutique locations include Palm Beach Gardens, Delray Beach, and Boca Raton in addition to Palm Beach.

COST: Prices vary.

PRO TIP: Lilly Pulitzer's Prints with Purpose spotlights charities such as First Tee–Palm Beaches by creating limited-edition designs and selling them to generate proceeds.

Lilly Pulitzer has blossomed to include athletic togs and swimsuits, beach towels and sunglasses, and home decor, hostess gifts, and stationery supplies.

A 30-something Lilly Pulitzer displays her vivid wares in a Palm Beach shop. Photo courtesy of Lilly Pulitzer

them up. With the addition of floral scenes, jungle animals, pluming peacocks, and other motifs to the patterns, the dresses started outselling the drinks. In 1959, the Lilly Pulitzer label was formed, and in 1961, it caught the eye of Jacqueline Kennedy. The day the first lady—who often went barefoot in the classic shift while at the Winter White House—appeared on the cover of *Life* magazine wearing one, the brand exploded.

PINK PARADISE

Who among the cultural and political illuminati gallivanted about the retreat?

Judy Garland, Lena Horne, and Frank Sinatra to name a few. The Supremes's Mary Wilson and actress Cicely Tyson often huddled in the old Polo Steaks & Seafood restaurant until closing time. Kitty Carlisle Hart, ever the entertainer, sang in the cabaret-themed Royal Room at age 93. (The property's then-publicist worried about the doyenne's actuarial odds until learning that she not only put on a fine performance but also proceeded to go out dancing with the master of ceremonies until way after midnight and awoke bright and early the next morning to swim laps.) Favorite Beatle John Lennon and Italian diva Sophia Loren stayed at the Colony Hotel and so did a duke, a duchess, a maharanee, a shah, a few kings, and several US presidents. Sir Winston Churchill's granddaughter, artist and part-time Palm Beach resident Edwina Sandys, hung several original paintings in the suites. Celebrity mascot Johnnie Brown is named after a pet monkey belonging to celebrity architect Addison Mizner, and the adorable animal's visage

THE COLONY HOTEL

WHAT: A regal resort with an unparalleled guest list

WHERE: 155 Hammon Ave.

COST: Nightly rates vary by season.

PRO TIP: The Colony Hotel's swimming pool has an unusual shape resembling the state of Florida minus the Panhandle.

When guest Judy Garland flew to Washington, DC, for John F. Kennedy's inauguration, she forgot her ball gown in the hotel closet, and the Air Force was deployed to retrieve it.

The Colony Hotel and its pastel paint pierce the sky.

can be spotted throughout the lobby. The past owner of the hotel was a sports illuminati. Robert Wetenhall, who died in 2021 at age 86, had a stake in the Boston (now New England) Patriots in the late 1960s.

PORTAL TO THE PAST

Why are millions of taxpayer dollars being used to repair a hole in the ground?

Constructed in 1961 on Peanut Island, the 1,500-square-foot nuclear-bomb shelter served as a top-secret hideout for the president during the Cuban Missile Crisis. The escalating confrontation between the Soviet Union and the United States raised the threat of war. Officials estimated that weapons launched by the Russians from the Caribbean nation would reach the Eastern Seaboard in minutes. The president had his Winter White House in Palm Beach, and protection was paramount. A tunnel, reinforced by corrugated metal, shielded by lead plates, and leading to a Quonset hut buried beneath 12 feet of dirt, guaranteed safety. In the event the president had to be rushed there, the room was equipped, outfitted, and stocked so that he could run the country until the emergency passed. The John F. Kennedy Fallout Bunker remained classified until 1974. In 1992, the Palm Beach Maritime Museum started giving tours of the site and its

JOHN F. KENNEDY FALLOUT BUNKER

WHAT: A Cold War–era safe room for the commander-in-chief

WHERE: Riviera Beach

COST: To be determined when restoration is completed

PRO TIP: Peanut Island can be accessed via shuttle boat from Riviera Beach Marina Village or the Sailfish Marina Resort as well as by private vessel.

The 1936 Coast Guard Boat House and Coast Guard Station House on Peanut Island are part of the John F. Kennedy Fallout Bunker restoration project.

The tunnel to the John F. Kennedy Fallout Bunker is 40 feet long. Photo by Willy Volk

doomsday objects—gas masks, Geiger counters, and K-rations. Deterioration, compounded by damage from hurricanes, shuttered the bunker in 2017. Palm Beach County reached an agreement in 2022 with the Port of Palm Beach, which owns Peanut Island, to manage the property and carry out a restoration project estimated to cost between $6 and $8 million so visitors can once again walk through history.

HUNTING GROUNDS

What draws shoppers far and wide to the downtown district?

Glossies such as *Architectural Digest*, *Art & Antiques*, and *House Beautiful* have knighted the strollable six-block space between Belvedere Road and Southern Boulevard in West Palm Beach as a leading destination for finicky finders. *Condé Nast Traveler* also Midas-touched the area by naming it one of the best places to explore in the United States. Decorators, designers, and devotees from all over the world frequent the more than 40 stores on Antique Row looking for pieces of history. Inside Flamingo Feather Interiors, Iconic Snob Galeries, the Elephant's Foot Antiques, and other outlets, objects that date from the 17th to the 20th centuries await. The art, furniture, jewelry, rugs, and more all have

ANTIQUE ROW

WHAT: A dream for die-hard collectors

WHERE: South Dixie Hwy., West Palm Beach

COST: Deals and steals can be had.

PRO TIP: Retail therapy and restaurants go hand in hand, and Belle & Maxwell's on the south end of Antique Row prepares Italian meals seven days a week.

Above: *Antique Row officially steps off at Monroe Drive.*

Opposite: *The Elephant's Foot Antiques has served customers since 1963. Photo courtesy of Marvin Ray*

tales to tell as do the stores. Iconic Snob Galeries is a 1940s-era building that used to be Electrolux. It went from selling high-end home appliances—Eureka, Tappan, and White-Westinghouse—to high-end home accents—Biedermeier, Gustavian, and Hollywood Regency. The Elephant's Foot derived its name from a childhood memory of the business's original owner. She used to have an old umbrella stand shaped like an elephant's foot in her bedroom, and it was the perfect place to hide toys she no longer wanted. The business's current owner kept the name, deciding it was fitting for a store housing items others no longer wanted.

Evening on Antique Row, a benefit for the Historical Society of Palm Beach County, hits the street every spring and turns South Dixie Highway into a pedestrian-friendly party zone.

DIGGING UP THE PAST

Whose dirty deeds are buried along with their bodies?

Lena Clarke, the murdering West Palm Beach postmistress, died in 1967 at age 81 more than four decades after confessing to fatally shooting her lover at an Orlando hotel. The sordid story began in 1918 when the service worker developed a bad habit of embezzling cash from the daily take instead of depositing it in the bank. She methodically tried to blame Fred Miltimore, a coworker with whom she was having an affair. In 1921, she made off with $42,000 (some accounts identify the amount as $31,000) and hightailed it to Orlando where Miltimore, who had since left the post office, relocated to run a restaurant. The deceitful thief lured Miltimore to her room, drugged him with a morphine pill, and put a bullet in his head. She then appeared at a nearby police station, told officers where Miltimore was, and insisted they arrest him for squandering the money. During the interrogation, the troubled preacher's daughter with a

WOODLAWN CEMETERY

WHAT: A city-operated graveyard with stories to tell

WHERE: 1301 S Dixie Hwy., West Palm Beach

COST: The cemetery is free to explore. Tours also are free with a suggested donation toward maintenance and upkeep.

PRO TIP: The gates are open from 7:30 a.m. to 3:30 p.m. daily, and tours take place on select full moons.

Historian Ginger Pedersen, who helps conduct tours of Woodlawn Cemetery, wrote a book about Lena Clarke titled the *Crystal Ball Chronicles: Lena Clarke's Twisted Tale of Love, Deception, and Crime.*

The concrete archway at the entrance to Woodlawn Cemetery reads, "That which is so universal as death must be a blessing." Photo courtesy of city of West Palm Beach

dark side—she believed she had 12 previous lives—confessed to both the killing and the stealing. The chilling account, which was sensationalized in newspapers across the county, is retold during lively full-moon tours of the cemetery that reveal eye-opening details about some of the others beneath the soil.

LEGEND OF THE SEAS

Why is Palm Beach named after a tropical fruit tree?

In 1878, a 175-ton Spanish brigantine traveling from the Western Caribbean ran aground off the Florida coast between Jupiter and Hypoluxo. The *Providencia* was on its way back to Europe lugging a supply of animal hides, Cuban rum, lumber, spices, and vegetables in addition to Trinidadian coconuts—20,000 of them. The smattering of settlers in the largely uninhabited area rushed to the beach. William Lanehart was one of the first to reach the vessel and ended up buying it from the insurance company. He and his friend Hiram Hammon gathered the coconuts and began selling them for pennies apiece. A little more than 1,000 were purchased while the rest were planted. In a few years, the tropical fruit tree became a ubiquitous sight on the island, inspiring its name.

Discover the Palm Beaches's annual Providencia Award celebration highlights and honors individuals and organizations for extraordinary contributions in furthering tourism in the region.

THE *PROVIDENCIA*

WHAT: A ship that started a town

WHERE: Providencia Park is at 1100 N Flagler Dr. in West Palm Beach

COST: Free to explore

PRO TIP: A grassy and spacious area with Intracoastal Waterway views, Providencia Park is perfect for a picnic.

Left: *The legend of the* Providencia *endures.*

Opposite: *Providencia Park is dotted with coconut-bearing palms.*

Providencia Park in West Palm Beach is dedicated to the historic wreck. Lanehart and Hammon continue to live on more than a century after their deaths. Lanehart was a skilled carpenter whose brother George Lainhart (they spelled their last names differently) established Lainhart & Potter, the oldest continuously operating business in the county until it closed in 2012. Hammon Avenue is the site of the Colony Hotel, a distinguished resort that attracted a who's who of celebrities in the 1950s and 1960s and is as illustrious now as it was then.

ONLY IN NATURE

What peculiar planting anchors the inner sanctum of the Eden?

Remarkable not only for its long, arched branches but also for its shapely fruit, the *Kigelia Africana*, commonly called the sausage tree, has a playful appearance that provokes laughs, legends, myths, and more. Its bearings can weigh as much as 20 pounds apiece and hang from cordlike vines that resemble giant pendulums. The Ndebele are said to symbolically bury them when a family member or a loved one dies. After proper drying and preparation, the pulp and seeds can be used to make a liquid substance intended to boost male fertility. In addition to its list of medicinal benefits—anti-inflammatory support, enhanced skin health, relief from infections, and treatment for malaria and rheumatism among them—interesting folklore surrounds the sausage tree. It is believed to have talismanic powers that ward off evil spirits. It is believed to have magical properties that bring abundance. It is believed to have sacred qualities that tribal cultures revere. Native to sub-Saharan savannas, it has influenced customs and traditions on the continent

THE SOCIETY OF THE FOUR ARTS DEMONSTRATION GARDEN

WHAT: The site of an unusual specimen

WHERE: 100 Four Arts Plz.

COST: Free to explore

PRO TIP: The half-acre area is divided into nine themed spaces including the Informal Garden, where the sausage tree is located.

The Garden Club of Palm Beach maintains the Society of the Four Arts Demonstration Garden, which is open from 10 a.m. to 5 p.m. daily.

The sausage tree is the largest tree in the Society of the Four Arts Demonstration Garden.

for centuries. All of the above aside, an important fact about the sausage tree is its value to the ecosystem. When in bloom, bell-shaped flowers with a less-than-pleasant scent attract bats, supporting the population of pollinators.

PALACE ON WHEELS

What piece of Florida history is preserved in the Henry Morrison Flagler Museum?

Railcar No. 91, Henry Morrison Flagler's oak-paneled coach, has been on display in the Beaux Arts–style building since 2005, giving guests a glimpse into the Gilded Age. Jackson & Sharp, of Wilmington, Delaware, built the coach in 1886, and the American industrialist commandeered it to survey his line. He rode Railcar No. 91 from Miami to Key West on January 22, 1902, and at the end of the 150-mile maiden voyage, thousands of cheering spectators greeted him to celebrate the completion of the Over-Sea Railroad. The Over-Sea Railroad represented an engineering feat so ambitious that critics coined it "Flagler's Folly." The day the train pulled into the station in the Southernmost City, supporters recoined it the "Eighth Wonder of the World." Railcar No. 91 was sold in 1935 to Georgia Northern Railway and again in 1949 to be used as housing for migrant farmworkers in Virginia. The Henry Morrison Flagler Museum acquired the coach in

FLAGLER KENAN PAVILION

WHAT: The staging area for Henry Morrison Flagler's main mode of transportation

WHERE: One Whitehall Way

COST: Fee for admission

PRO TIP: The museum has tea service in the Flagler Kenan Pavilion from November to May, plating sandwiches, scones, and sweets on fine Whitehall china.

The Flagler Kenan Pavilion recognizes William Rand Kenan Jr., the engineer brother of Henry Morrison Flagler's third wife, Mary Lily Kenan, who helped build the Over-Sea Railroad.

Above: *Henry Morrison Flagler's desk and sitting room are in pristine condition.*

Left: *Railcar No. 91, at rest on the tracks, is showcased in a palatial, light-filled train station. Photos courtesy of Henry Morrison Flagler Museum*

1959, one year before opening to the public, and exhibited it on the south lawn until the Flagler Kenan Pavilion was assembled to accommodate the artifact. Railcar No. 91's ornate office and sitting room, well-appointed primary suite and guest berths, and iron oven and stove all have been restored to their original appearance.

ENTERTAINMENT ENCLAVE

Why has the theater that once drew A-listers to its stage been dark since 2004?

The well-known waterfront venue suffered from years of neglect long before it was shuttered for unsafe conditions. When the curtain finally closed, the building sat empty and in need of an operator for nearly two decades. All the while, the infrastructure continued to fail until it was rendered obsolete. A major upgrade was in order. Poor economic conditions in 2008 slowed plans for a renovation. Finally, in 2014, a development company stepped in and signed a lease to save the Palm Beach landmark. Following a transformational overhaul, the Royal Poinciana Playhouse has returned to its Regency-style opulence. While sightings of Bing Crosby, Zsa Zsa Gabor, Jackie Gleason, Bob Hope, Ginger Rogers, and other regulars at the playhouse's raucous Celebrity Room are mere memories, the trompe l'oeil ceiling mural beneath which they

ROYAL POINCIANA PLAYHOUSE

WHAT: A high-society hub of comedy, film, music, and more

WHERE: 70 Royal Poinciana Way

COST: Ticket prices vary.

PRO TIP: The Royal Poinciana Playhouse anchors the Royal Poinciana Plaza, an oasis of fashion, food, and fun.

The Royal Poinciana Playhouse features a large lobby with a grand piano, a performing-arts hall with 400 seats, and 12,000 square feet of retail space.

Above: *The Royal Poinciana Playhouse, shown here as it appeared in 1959, underwent an extensive overhaul.*

Left: *The entrance to the Royal Poinciana Playhouse featured a preppy canopy. Photos from Library of Congress*

drank, dined, and danced has been preserved. A new restaurant occupying the storied spot retains the authenticity of the swanky bar-and-lounge scene and marks the town's first public eating establishment on the Intracoastal Waterway. The most familiar part of the playhouse, the curved east facade, has been preserved as well. The four Roman statues atop the architectural element were placed in storage when construction began and, to the delight of patrons, stand watch once more.

SEASIDE SPLENDOR

Whose hand-painted portraits envelop one of the idyllic hotel's event spaces?

Juan Ponce de León, the Spanish conquistador who discovered Florida, fills one of 44 niches lining the decadently detailed, diagonally patterned plaster ceiling embellished with 260 cherubs in the Gold Room. The frescoes glow with color depictions of Old World explorers and Renaissance rulers. Alfred Crimi, an Italian American artist trained at New York's National Academy of Design and Beaux-Arts de Paris, created each of them. Crimi's renderings of Marco Polo, Christopher Columbus, Leonardo da Vinci, Ferdinand Magellan, Galileo Galilei, and other figures from the 13th through the 17th centuries provide a hovering history lesson. Seeing the faces of those who conquered, engineered, navigated, and theorized their way through the ages, laying the foundation for modern society, makes the 50-square-foot chamber feel more like a museum than a meeting hall. Four framed informational guides referencing the north, south, east, and west walls identify the

Dramatic underlighting does the frescoes justice.

THE BREAKERS PALM BEACH

WHAT: A five-star accommodation on the beach

WHERE: One S County Rd.

COST: Nightly rates vary by season.

PRO TIP: The Breakers Palm Beach's Seafood Bar has the ocean as a backdrop and an aquarium as a countertop and is worth stopping by for a drink.

Juan Ponce de León lived from 1460 to 1521.

frescoes by number, image, and biography. The Gold Room, lingering behind three sets of double doors past the Breakers Palm Beach's lobby, replicates Venice's Gallerie Accademia, an institution housed in the Santa Maria della Carità church and school buildings in Italy. Its other attributes are an elaborately carved fireplace and mantle and two symbolic tapestries titled *Country Scenes* and the *Story of Anthony and Cleopatra.*

The Breakers Palm Beach, named one of Fortune Media's 100 best companies to work for, is owned by descendants of Henry Morrison Flagler.

TASTY WAVES

Why does the spot at the north tip of the island make riders say "cowabunga"?

When conditions are good, the curved shoreline that meets the jetty south of the Palm Beach Inlet offers excellent surfing. Heavy tubes in shallow water yield an epic yet tricky experience as the ride can result in broken boards for the not-too-cautious. The lineup comprises, for the most part, a small group of locals who have been faithful to Reef Road for decades. They discovered the site's potential in the late 1960s while longboarding across its awesome ocean dynamics at a time when surfing was coming into its own. Former Palm Beacher Jimmy Buffett frequently windmilled his way out to the action. The lack of access—Reef Road does not have public parking and is in a residential area—adds to the allure. Things work best with a strong swell from the northeast and prevailing winds in the same direction, narrowing the window to the winter months and their ideal weather patterns. When firing, the 15-footers that wash ashore are hollow, powerful, and imposing, and

REEF ROAD

WHAT: A shreddable stretch of sand and sea

WHERE: North of Dolphin Rd. and south of Onondaga Ave.

COST: Free to explore

PRO TIP: Because of its propensity to produce big Atlantic rollers, Reef Road is recommended for those experienced in the sport.

Because Reef Road does not have public parking and is in a residential area, surfers must arrive by bicycle, by foot, by skateboard, by Uber, etc.

A cloudless, windless day at Reef Road beckons.

rival the monsters at well-known beaches and breaks around the world. Those who successfully pop up and take off will be sittin' on top of the world, to quote the Beach Boys.

MORE THAN A DOT ON THE MAP

What distinction does the tiny town have that no other place in Florida can claim?

Those who sink their toes in the sand between Bamboo Road and the Palm Beach Inlet do so at the easternmost point in the state. Here, the Gulf Stream and its fertile current come closest to the peninsula, making for excellent fishing—grouper and snapper are plentiful year-round—and enjoyable swimming—the warm flow creates pleasant and plunge-friendly ocean temperatures and clear, blue-green waters. Anchoring the easternmost point is a hulking piece of industrial equipment called the pump house. The pump house functions as a vacuum for sand that accumulates on the north side of the inlet, funneling the buildup through a buried pipe that resurfaces on the south side to distribute it onto the beach. The odd structure has been part of the scenery since 1958. At the Sailfish Marina Resort, the easternmost point emulates the southernmost city every Thursday with a take on Key West's fabled Sunset Celebration. Its geographical distinction aside,

PALM BEACH SHORES

WHAT: A one-quarter-square-mile community by the sea

WHERE: Town Hall is at 247 Edwards Ln.

COST: Free to explore

PRO TIP: Palm Beach Shores is home to the recently revamped Buccaneer Waterfront Bar and Grill, a postwar bastion of booze that had been closed since the early 2000s.

Left: *Decorative pavers signal the beginning of the pedestrian parkway.*

Opposite: *The pump house was built in 1958.*

Palm Beach Shores is most proud of its Tree City USA distinction. The Arbor Day Foundation recognized the town for its display of figs, gumbo limbos, queen palms, and additional species along a pedestrian parkway that begins at the fountain and ends at the pavilion. The town celebrates its status each March by planting a new sapling.

Gen Xers heedlessly climbed the arm of the pump house, some making it to the end, and daringly jumped into the shallow surf for fun.

POWER COUPLE

What billion-dollar brand did the husband-and-wife hairdressing team invent?

Now part of the L'Oréal USA Professional Products Division, Matrix owes its existence to Arnold and Sydell Miller. The suave stylist and the energetic entrepreneur established the company in 1980, introducing a line of high-end hair-coloring and hair-texturizing options to help those behind the chair improve their techniques and make clients look and feel their best. The Millers eventually added shampoos, conditioners, foams, gels, serums, sprays, and spritzes to the mix for home use so clients could maintain their hair on their own. One of their formulations, Biolage, entered the market in 1990. The brainchild of Arnold Miller, it blended biology with modern science and resulted in a signature fragrance using natural ingredients. Sydell Miller's business acumen brought Biolage's instantly recognizable white bottles to salons across the country. Their love story began in 1957, when she went to get her hair done at his shop in Cleveland. He asked her out on the spot. One week later, he proposed. Their success led them to buy a home in Palm Beach like other

ARNOLD AND SYDELL MILLER

WHAT: Sydell Miller's gobsmacking estate

WHERE: La Rêverie is at 1415 S Ocean Blvd.

COST: Not for sale

PRO TIP: A recent appraisal valued La Rêverie at $220 million.

In 2001, Sydell Miller's new Palm Beach home was completed, and when she sold La Rêverie in 2019, the 10-bedroom, 14-bathroom French-style classic fetched $105 million.

Arnold and Sydell Miller show off their Matrix collection. Photo courtesy of the Miller family

affluent achievers. Arnold Miller died in 1992 at age 60. Sydell Miller took over as CEO of Matrix until its sale in 1994 and retired in 1996. A supporter of local causes ranging from the arts to women's rights, she died in 2024 at age 86.

ARTIST EXTRAORDINAIRE

What is the retired member of Metallica doing in the Sunshine State?

The Rock & Roll Hall of Fame inductee and six-time Grammy Award recipient who slapped the bass for 15 years with fellow headbangers James Hetfield and Lars Ulrich started slapping paint on the wall when he relocated to Jupiter Inlet Colony in 2019. Jason Newsted's first mural, *Evolution of Tequesta*, lit up an alley behind a restaurant. The swirling colors and crazy shapes intertwining throughout the 12-by-22-foot piece told the story of Native American tribes such as the Ais, Jaega, and Jobe that once inhabited the area around the small coastal village. Newsted's second mural glows in the dark on the side of the Lighthouse ArtCenter Gallery & School of Art's 3D Studio building. It is a similarly sized assault of images, letters, numbers, phrases, and symbols that speak to its theme and its title, *Art is the Center of the Earth*. Prior to parting ways with Metallica, the career musician founded the thrash group Flotsam and Jetsam and also toured with "Prince of Darkness" Ozzy Osbourne. Since moving to Florida, the

JASON NEWSTED

WHAT: A riotous acrylic on concrete

WHERE: 395 Seabrook Rd., Tequesta

COST: Free to view

PRO TIP: The vision of the Lighthouse ArtCenter Gallery & School of Art is to deepen ties with and enrich the lives of an inclusive community through art.

Jason Newsted's Chophouse Band cranks out the tunes most frequently at the Lighthouse ArtCenter Gallery & School of Art during benefit concerts for the cultural nonprofit.

Above: Art is the Center of the Earth *took 130 hours to complete.*

Left: *Jason Newsted makes his point both literally and figuratively.*

power-chord-belting axman has toned it down and plays mostly acoustic guitar with his Chophouse Band, singing lead on an assortment of American bluegrass and folk hits by Johnny Cash, Tom Petty, and Neil Young. All of the shows are fundraisers.

BACK TO BASICS

What was it like to attend school more than a century ago?

Pupils in late-1800s America studied reading, writing, and arithmetic in one-room buildings much like Laura Ingalls in *Little House on the Prairie*. Fans of the 1970s television show recall the daughter of Charles and Caroline showing up bright and early for "Miss Beadle" in Plum Creek near Walnut Grove, Minnesota. During the same time period, children in Palm Beach County toted their textbooks and their lunch tins to the Little Red Schoolhouse, a 22-by-40-foot space on the Lake Trail north of the Royal Poinciana Bridge. Constructed in 1886, it was the first educational institution in South Florida. The teacher was Hattie Gale, who at 16 was younger than some of those she instructed. The school operated until 1901 and then was abandoned for a four-room site near West Palm Beach's Clematis Street. In 1960, the Gardeners Society of Palm Beach refurbished the deteriorating, dormant structure, and it was moved to Phipps Ocean Park. Since 1990, the Preservation Foundation of Palm Beach has swung open the strap-hinged double doors of the Little Red Schoolhouse to fourth-graders participating in the living-history

Above: *Lumber for the Little Red Schoolhouse arrived on a schooner from Jacksonville.*

Opposite: *The Little Red Schoolhouse is a Florida Heritage Site.*

program. The program exposes youths to the pioneer way of life through biographical role-playing, period dress—bonnets and pinafores for the girls and caps and suspenders for the boys—and exercises in Spencerian script.

LITTLE RED SCHOOLHOUSE

WHAT: A rusty shed saved for posterity

WHERE: 356 S County Rd.

COST: Free to view

PRO TIP: A major redesign of Phipps Ocean Park entailed relocating the Little Red Schoolhouse to higher, less flood-prone ground.

Because the Little Red Schoolhouse's living-history program is a reenactment, students are encouraged to bring authentic food—cold porridge and cured meat, for example—or fruits and vegetables grown in South Florida.

THE LITTLE ENGINE THAT COULD

Where can fragments of the abandoned track be seen?

A section of rail, sleepers, fasteners, and ballast is preserved neatly on the grass at Town Hall Park in Juno Beach. The Celestial Railroad Historical Plaque explains the genesis of the Jupiter and Lake Worth Railway and how it changed the lives of early residents by providing much-needed transportation between the inlet and the north end of the present-day Intracoastal Waterway. The seven-and-a-half-mile link carried goods to paddle-wheel steamers that then carried them to consumers in Palm Beach and areas to the south. The train had two passenger coaches in addition to its freight cars and shuttled a growing population of settlers from terminus to terminus. The railway was so convenient and, more importantly, essential that the half-hour trip cost riders 75 cents apiece, a pretty penny. It operated from 1889 to 1895, and its route ran through the same spot as the display in the park. Interestingly,

CELESTIAL RAILROAD

WHAT: A narrow-gauge line that historians describe as the smallest in the world

WHERE: 841 Ocean Dr., Juno Beach

COST: Free to explore

PRO TIP: In addition to the Celestial Railroad Historical Plaque in Town Hall Park, there is a Celestial Railroad Historical Marker in Loggerhead Park.

The Celestial Railroad is one of 25 stops on the Discover Juno Beach tour, a self-guided route outlined at juno-beach.fl.us/history and accessible via the PocketSights app.

Top: *Town Hall Park also marks the location of the original Juno Beach Town Hall that stood from 1961 to 1991. Photo courtesy of Juno Beach Historical Society*

Bottom: *Several streets in Juno Beach reflect the theme of the Celestial Railroad with names like Apollo Drive and Neptune Road. Photo from Library of Congress*

the locomotive permanently pointed south and had to travel in reverse to go north. Because its two stations were called Jupiter and Juno, and its two stops were called Venus and Mars, someone dubbed it the Celestial Railroad in reference to the 1843 story by Nathaniel Hawthorne. The name stuck. The short-lived enterprise succumbed to Henry Morrison Flagler's Florida East Coast Railway and was sold at a public auction.

SALTY PIECE OF LAND

For whom is the condominium-covered cay named?

One of the more than two dozen children fathered by Issac Singer, of sewing-machine fame, Paris Singer first visited Palm Beach in 1917, renting a cottage on Peruvian Avenue and using some of his inheritance to buy land during the boom. He met and befriended architect Addison Mizner, whom he would persuade to move to the area one year later. By that time, Singer had acquired parcels on both the north and south sides of the Palm Beach Inlet and offered Mizner a lifelong retainer to build hotels. Two were planned north of the inlet on what became known as Singer Island. Construction began on the Blue Heron Hotel—a 36-hole golf course was among its amenities—although work progressed no further than the service wing. The Paris Singer Hotel never came to fruition.

While married, Paris Singer had an affair with trailblazing dancer Isadora Duncan that resulted in the birth of a son who drowned in the Seine River.

Singer Island stretches for three miles along the Atlantic Ocean.

The hurricane of 1928 and the Great Depression of 1929 ended Singer's real-estate career and his relationship with Mizner. Singer died in 1932 at age 65. The unfinished Blue Heron Hotel stood for more than a decade after his death until it was demolished. The Blue Heron Bridge, a high-rise span that connects Singer Island to the mainland, and Blue Heron Boulevard, the road that leads up to it, are references to the failed project.

SINGER ISLAND

WHAT: A tropical paradise where Paris Singer took his friends for parties and picnics

WHERE: Riviera Beach

COST: Free to explore

PRO TIP: The Islander Grill & Tiki Bar, a fun poolside hang south of the municipal beach, serves frothy and/or frozen concoctions in take-home glasses.

Paris Singer. Photo from Wikimedia Commons

LEAKY TEEPEE

Whom did crowds wait in line to see at the entertainment complex?

From hair bands to Harry Connick Jr., from country twanger Reba McEntire to classic violinist Itzhak Perlman, and from ice-skating shows to tractor pulls, the bright-white venue across the street from the Palm Beach Mall oozed with fun. The Ringling Bros. and Barnum & Bailey Circus, billed as the Greatest Show on Earth and starring animal trainer extraordinaire Gunther Gebel-Williams, came to town every year. World Wrestling Federation rumblers André the Giant, "Rowdy" Roddy Piper, and Dusty Rhodes made Monday nights less mundane. Peter Wolf sang "Centerfold," "Freeze-Frame," and "Love Stinks" to J. Geils's guitar during an epic show that U2, not yet an arena powerhouse, opened. On February 13, 1977, Elvis Presley entered the building. Wearing his Blue Rainfall Jumpsuit, the "King of Rock 'n' Roll" started with "See See Rider" and ended with "Can't Help Falling in Love," performing medleys of other big hits in between during a one-hour set. He died six months later. For more than three decades, the West Palm Beach Auditorium had a constantly changing marquee offering something for everyone. The fact that its weird, pointy roof often was breached by rain did not deter a generation of South Floridians from going to shows.

WEST PALM BEACH AUDITORIUM

WHAT: A celebrated arena now owned by a religious organization

WHERE: 1610 Palm Beach Lakes Blvd., West Palm Beach

COST: Free to visit

PRO TIP: The West Palm Beach Auditorium's heyday began on Labor Day of 1967 and ended in 1998 when the city sold it to the Jehovah's Witnesses.

Above: *The West Palm Beach Auditorium now is the West Palm Beach Christian Convention Center.*

Left: *The boys from Pasadena, California, loaded in July 6, 1979. Photos courtesy of Susie Best*

With a striking resemblance to Disney World's Space Mountain, the West Palm Beach Auditorium was shaped by Chicago architect Bertrand Goldberg, who designed the Windy City's conspicuous corn-cob buildings.

TAKE ME OUT TO THE BALL GAME

When were the initial Spring Training bouts in West Palm Beach?

In 1924, the first pitch was thrown at Municipal Field, where preseason matchups for the Cincinnati Reds and the New York Yankees set South Florida on a course to be a destination for professional baseball. Municipal Field became Wright Field in 1927, honoring City Manager George Wright, and drew the Philadelphia Athletics and the St. Louis Browns. In 1952, Wright Field was renamed Connie Mack Field for the player whose career began in 1886 behind home plate with the Washington Nationals. He was inducted into the National Baseball Hall of Fame in 1937 and retired 13 years later as the Athletics's business suit–wearing manager. In 1963, Spring Training moved to a new facility, the West Palm Beach Municipal Stadium, home of the Boston (later Atlanta) Braves and the Montreal Expos. The old Connie Mack Field now is

CONNIE MACK FIELD

WHAT: An action-packed sports locale lost to development

WHERE: 701 Okeechobee Blvd., West Palm Beach

COST: Free to explore

PRO TIP: Former US Sen. Connie Mack III, who from 1989 to 2001 represented Florida, is Connie Mack's grandson.

Cornelius Alexander McGillicuddy, who also wore jerseys for the Buffalo Bisons and the Pittsburgh Pirates, shortened his name to Connie Mack so it would fit on scoreboards.

Above: *Old photographs of Connie Mack Field can be found on level 1 of the Kravis Center's parking garage.*

Left: *Fans who can hunt down the monument are invited to take an air swing.*

the site of the Kravis Center's parking garage. Behind the service entrance, in a shallow ditch, lies a hard-to-find monument that marks the exact location where Joe DiMaggio, Lou Gehrig, Mickey Mantle, Jackie Robinson, Babe Ruth, and Ted Williams stepped up to bat. As for West Palm Beach Municipal Stadium, the last pitch was thrown March 26, 1997, and it now is the site of a Home Depot.

FORMIDABLE FIR

What gimmick did the gossip magazine use to garner attention?

Everyone loved the supermarket tabloid during the holidays. When December arrived, parents loaded their children into the family car and hit the road for Lantana to behold the largest decorated tree in the country. With their heads tilted back, they smiled at the sight of thousands of twinkling lights, hundreds of colorful bows, strands of garland nearly one mile long, and a giant star trimming the 125-footer. That month, the scandal sheet whose headlines ridiculed celebrities and warned of aliens stopped traffic on Route 1 as lines of cars pilgrimaged to the festive scene. A nativity display, an old-fashioned sleigh, and the sound of carols also were part of the extravaganza that attracted tens of millions of onlookers, more than the number of readers who bought the issue with Elvis Presley in an open casket on the cover. The tradition began in 1971 when Generoso Pope Jr. moved the New York–based paper to Palm Beach County. It ended in 1988 when the publisher died at age 61. One Christmas, Burt Reynolds, the legendary actor whose personal business was fodder for the *National Enquirer*, exacted revenge. He collected horse manure from his ranch in nearby Jupiter and transported it onto a helicopter that hovered above the tree while bombing the boughs below.

NATIONAL ENQUIRER

WHAT: A supersized symbol that made the *Guinness Book of World Records*

WHERE: 600 S East Coast Ave., Lantana

COST: Now the location of the Palm Beach Maritime Academy's Upper School Campus, the site is free to visit.

PRO TIP: West Palm Beach is the place to be during the most wonderful time of the year when a 35-foot tree sculpted from 700 tons of sand is unveiled on the Great Lawn.

The National Enquirer *Christmas Tree came from Canada, and it took a train, a freighter, and a truck to get it to Lantana. Photo courtesy of Susie Best*

By comparison, the Rockefeller Center Christmas Tree in New York averages 75 feet, and the tallest one in its history was a 100-footer in 1999.

METAL MASTERPIECE

Who conceptualized the installation at the Mandel Jewish Community Center?

The progenitor of kineticism, Yaacov Agam explores an art form that represents movement and progress and relies on the role of the viewer. His "Agamographs" hinge on the angle, direction, and position from which they are seen, challenging onlookers with a call to action. *Menorah* richly represents his breakthrough lenticular style. At 10 feet tall and nine panels wide, the geometric spectacle has enlivened the grounds of the Mandel Jewish Community Center since 1993. Agam supervised its placement on the Palm Beach Gardens campus and attended the dedication ceremony. Born in 1928 to Orthodox parents, Agam pursued his passion by leaning toward a nonrepresentational aesthetic in order to stay true to his faith, which prohibits graven images. He took courses at the Bezalel Academy of Arts and Design in Jerusalem and studied with renowned Bauhaus color theorist Johannes Itten in Switzerland.

Yaacov Agam belongs to an elite list of accomplished artists, Salvador Dalí among them, who have a museum named in their honor.

MENORAH

WHAT: An incredible optical illusion of a sculpture

WHERE: 5221 Hood Rd., Palm Beach Gardens

COST: Free to view

PRO TIP: *Menorah* is disassembled every June—it is put into storage for safekeeping during hurricane season—and is reassembled in early December.

Above: Menorah *can be admired during the Mandel Jewish Community Center's operating hours. Photo by Ben Hoffman*

Opposite: *Yaacov Agam inventively signed* Menorah.

In 1951, he moved to Paris and met an art historian and expert in the Surrealist movement who introduced the 20-something to Salvador Dalí. Agam now was on the international stage. His 70-plus-year career has yielded hundreds of works in locations all over the world, and in 2017, the Yaacov Agam Museum of Art opened in his hometown of Rishon LeZion, Israel.

FABLED FELLOWSHIP

What hallmark contest does the West Palm Beach Fishing Club produce in the middle of winter?

The Silver Sailfish Derby, billed as the world's oldest, rolls around in January when South Florida shamelessly shows off with the warmest weather in the country. The tournament began in 1935 as leaders of the newly established West Palm Beach Fishing Club brainstormed ways to help the region regain its robust economy during the Great Depression. More than 90 years later, the eagerly anticipated event attracts anglers from colder climes wanting to get in on some of the best offshore action along the Eastern Seaboard. Boston Red Sox left-fielder Ted Williams and pro golfer Sam Snead had a long-standing rivalry at the tournament that became known as the Sailfish Grudge Match. Esteemed author Ernest Hemingway not only participated but also sponsored a trophy. The Silver Sailfish Derby has changed from its early days as an individual competition that lasted a

TIGHT LINES

WHAT: One of the oldest and most successful fishing organizations in existence

WHERE: 201 Fifth St., West Palm Beach

COST: Free to visit

PRO TIP: The club produces two other contests—the Palm Beach Tuna Tournament in the spring and the Full Moon Wahoo Series in the summer.

The club's charitable affiliate, the Palm Beach County Fishing Foundation, takes hundreds of children out on the water every year and educates them about the importance of marine preservation.

Above: *Mounts and memorabilia make up most of the inside space. Photo by Ted Swoboda*

Left: *The original building, now dwarfed by high-rises, made the National Register of Historic Places in 2016. Photo courtesy of West Palm Beach Fishing Club*

few months to a structured, two-day team outing capped at 50 boats. What has remained constant, though, is the awarding of the Mrs. Henry R. Rea prize, named for a former member's wife, to the winner with the most catch-and-releases. The West Palm Beach Fishing Club has grown to 1,600 cardholders and thrives as a conservation-conscious community of those who love the sport.

DEAL OR NO DEAL

Who wants to be a millionaire?

Developers dying to get their hands on seaside property have courted residents of a coveted community of mobile homes for years. In 2007, a $510 million offer to buy Briny Breezes went viral. Owners, some of whom purchased their pieces of paradise decades ago for less than $40,000, would have walked with nearly $1 million each. When the corporate board of directors had a financial dispute with Ocean Land Investments, the sale fell through. In 2023, the Kolter Group dangled $502 million in front of one of the last neighborhoods of its kind in the state. The board not only nixed the price but also doubled down by saying its 43 acres bounded by the Atlantic and the Intracoastal was worth $1 billion. In both instances, those living in the 488 manufactured houses breathed a collective sigh of relief. Chuck Swift, whose unit is on North Heron Drive, told local newspaper the *Coastal Star*, "Without question, Briny Breezes is unduplicable." While there is no guard gate, the area is private, and anyone who

BRINY BREEZES

WHAT: A trailer park with a view whose occupants are playing hard to get

WHERE: 5000 N Ocean Blvd.

COST: Free to explore

PRO TIP: Briny Breezes has its own town council, town manager, and town clerk in addition to the corporate board of directors that owns the lots.

The Briny Breezes Marina, the Briny Breezes Oceanfront Clubhouse, and the Briny Breezes Waterfront Pool and Cabana are among the amenities available to "Briny-ites" as residents are called.

Briny Breezes has 630 feet of private shoreline. Photo by Jerry Lower

parks a vehicle on-site needs to have an ID badge. Adding to its cause célèbre, interested parties wanting to move in must offer a minimum price, per the board, prior to entering into discussions.

VIVID VEGETATION

How many pieces of greenery grow from the side of a building?

Nearly 11,000 plants form a cascading curvilinear collage of lushness on the west face of the Esplanade. The luxury retail plaza's 840-square-foot concrete canvas brims with verdant layers of mondo grass, silver saw palmetto, Xanadu philodendron, and eight more leafy textures that add another alluring aspect to the already opulent Worth Avenue shopping scene. The first of its kind in the county when it was erected in 2010, the living wall is built into a professional paneling system specially engineered to withstand high winds. It comprises a series of one-by-one-foot squares filled with a soil alternative that retains water and does not erode. An around-the-clock computer-monitoring system tracks moisture levels and temperature ranges and employs zoned drip irrigation. A local landscape-design firm executed the project, making a point to take into account the architectural style of Addison Mizner, to whom Worth Avenue and much of Palm Beach owes its beauty, as well as the history of the tropical fruit tree that

LIVING WALL

WHAT: A much-photographed vertical garden

WHERE: 150 Worth Ave.

COST: Free to view

PRO TIP: The dusty miller adds a touch of frosty white to the living wall while the tradescantia Zebrina adds a touch of deep purple.

The hearty species on the living wall were propagated at a nursery for five months prior to their installation, a process that took four days.

The living wall is 35 feet wide and 24 feet high. Photo by Jean Matthews

named the island (the coconut palm). The living wall, sponsored by the Garden Club of Palm Beach as part of its town-beautification mission, has changed and evolved over time, and that is part of its appeal as a work of photosynthetic art.

EMPTY GRAVES

Where are Curtis and Marjorie Chillingworth laid to rest?

A crooked headstone memorializes a local circuit court judge and his wife at Woodlawn Cemetery in West Palm Beach. The monument, with its etched names and hyphenated years, has been shifted by the sands of time at the burial site, yet there are no bodies beneath it. Curtis and Marjorie Chillingworth were brazenly killed by guns for hire on a June morning in 1955. Curtis Chillingworth heard a knock on the door of his beach cottage in Manalapan, and when he opened it, a pair of hitmen rushed in, grabbed him and Marjorie Chillingworth, and forced them onto a boat. As they propelled out to sea, the hitmen tied weights around the victims and tossed them overboard. Their corpses were never recovered. The man who orchestrated the assassination, Joseph Peel, was a local municipal court judge who had been disciplined by his superior for unethical conduct and faced disbarment. The bad blood provided motive. Peel was convicted and sentenced to life in prison, where he died in

MURDER AND MAYHEM

WHAT: The Chillingworth plot

WHERE: 1301 S Dixie Hwy., West Palm Beach

COST: Free to explore

PRO TIP: Chillingworth Park off South Chillingworth Drive was named in honor of the slain husband and wife and the rest of their family.

> In the moments leading up to the drownings, with the boat idling four miles offshore, Floyd "Lucky" Holzapfel announced as he pushed Marjorie Chillingworth into the ocean, "Ladies first."

The terrifying deaths of the Chillingworths are recounted during tours of Woodlawn Cemetery in West Palm Beach. Photo by Ginger Pederson

1982 at age 57. The hitmen, Floyd "Lucky" Holzapfel and Bobby Lincoln, testified they "did it for Joe." Holzapfel died in 1996 at age 72, and Lincoln died in 2004 at age 79. The Chillingworths—Curtis was 58, and Marjorie was 47—were declared legally deceased in 1957.

ALTITUDINOUS EXPERIENCE

How high is the hill?

Few realize that a named peak exists in a sprawling preserve on the north side of the Palm Beach County line. Hikers can climb Hobe Mountain by following a boardwalk that takes them to an altitude of 86 feet, the steepest natural point south of Lake Okeechobee. There, an observation tower rises an additional 27 feet, scenically overlooking the Atlantic Ocean and the Intracoastal Waterway. Located in Jonathan Dickinson State Park, the ancient dune was shaped by rising and falling sea levels, crashing waves, and wind gusts that dynamically formed a dry, sandy coastal ridge. A community of heat-tolerant plants flourishes in the desert-like conditions of the Florida scrub ecosystem. Low-profile bushes bearing needles, spines, and thorns emit harsh odors and volatile oils to prevent wildlife from ingesting them. Inhabitants include the Florida scrub jay, a blue-headed, blue-winged, blue-tailed bird that is

HOBE MOUNTAIN

WHAT: An unusual elevation in a flat state

WHERE: 16450 Federal Hwy., Hobe Sound

COST: Fee for admission

PRO TIP: Hobe Mountain is one mile north of the ranger station on Park Road and can be seen from US Highway 1.

The observation tower, built in 1966, is undergoing significant repairs and restorations to meet safety standards, for which the Friends of Jonathan Dickinson State Park is raising money.

The boardwalk leading to the observation tower is 700 feet long. Photo courtesy of the Friends of Jonathan Dickinson State Park

federally endangered, and the Florida scrub lizard, identifiable by thick brown stripes running down each side of its body. Among the other flora and fauna that can be observed at Hobe Mountain are the "Dancing Lady" orchid—its bottom petals resemble a spinning skirt—and the burrowing gopher tortoise, a keystone species whose burrows provide shelter for hundreds of other animals. All are endemic to the slowly vanishing environment.

CLASS ACT

What's in a name?

The major benefactor of a regional center poised to become a national force in the performing arts has a background as diverse as the award-winning shows the stage produces. Milton Maltz, born in 1929 in South Bend, Indiana, started voicing radio dramas as a child shortly after his family moved to Chicago, where a schoolteacher encouraged him to audition. When television arrived, he started appearing on the air. After graduating from the University of Illinois with a bachelor's degree in journalism, he took a job at the National Security Agency and developed an interest in espionage. Then he started a communications company that bought and sold broadcast entities, including WMMS-FM, a classic-rock station in Cleveland that he turned into the flagship Buzzard 100.7. Using his juice, he helped bring the Rock & Roll Hall of Fame to the city. In 1998, he turned to philanthropy, opening the International Spy Museum in Washington, DC, to give the public an understanding of the

MALTZ JUPITER THEATRE

WHAT: The largest facility of its kind in the lower half of the United States

WHERE: 1001 E Indiantown Rd., Jupiter

COST: Ticket prices vary.

PRO TIP: The Jupiter Beach Resort & Spa, across the street from the Maltz Jupiter Theatre, has an oceanfront bar and restaurant that are convenient before or after shows.

The Maltz Jupiter Theatre underwent a series of significant expansions beginning in 2020 and now produces Broadway-caliber musicals and plays beneath a dazzling proscenium arch.

Milton Maltz. Photo courtesy of Maltz Jupiter Theatre

importance of the intelligence community. When he and his wife Tamar first visited Palm Beach, they decided to invest in what used to be the Burt Reynolds Dinner Theatre, a landmark venue that had fallen into financial trouble. Revitalized as the Maltz Jupiter Theatre, it seats 659 at its main stage and 198 at its second stage.

TITAN OF TECHNOLOGY

In which city was the world's first personal computer invented?

The birth of the PC took place in Boca Raton. With a code name of Acorn, the covert engineering feat resulted in the development of the direct-to-consumer product in 1981. The small team assigned to the task plucked resources from Intel, Microsoft, Zenith, and others to form a system with open architecture. In 1983, *Time* magazine named the industry-dawning 5150 "Machine of the Year." The odyssey of International Business Machines began in 1911 with the merger of three data-processing providers to form the Computing-Tabulating-Recording Company. In 1914, Thomas Watson Sr. joined as general manager and later CEO, renaming the firm and establishing its simple yet sweeping slogan, "THINK." Operations were based in Endicott, New York. IBM's second CEO, Thomas Watson Jr., put Boca Raton on the map when he moved the plant to a 550-acre site west of Interstate 95 and south of Yamato Road. The 3.6-million-square-foot building designed by powerhouse architect Marcel Breuer opened in 1967 and began manufacturing the System/360, the predecessor of the 5150. The ultimate keyboard command—Ctrl, Alt, Delete—was invented there. IBM sold the property in 1996, and it was rebranded as the Boca Raton Innovation Campus. Plans for a modern-day live-work-play village idled until a commercial real-estate group acquired the campus in 2018 and moved forward with the transformation.

INTERNATIONAL BUSINESS MACHINES

WHAT: An office complex whose Y-shapes and rectilinear structures embody brutalism

WHERE: 5000 T-Rex Ave., Boca Raton

COST: Free to explore

PRO TIP: The Boca Raton Innovation Campus has the longest hallway in the western hemisphere at more than 900 feet.

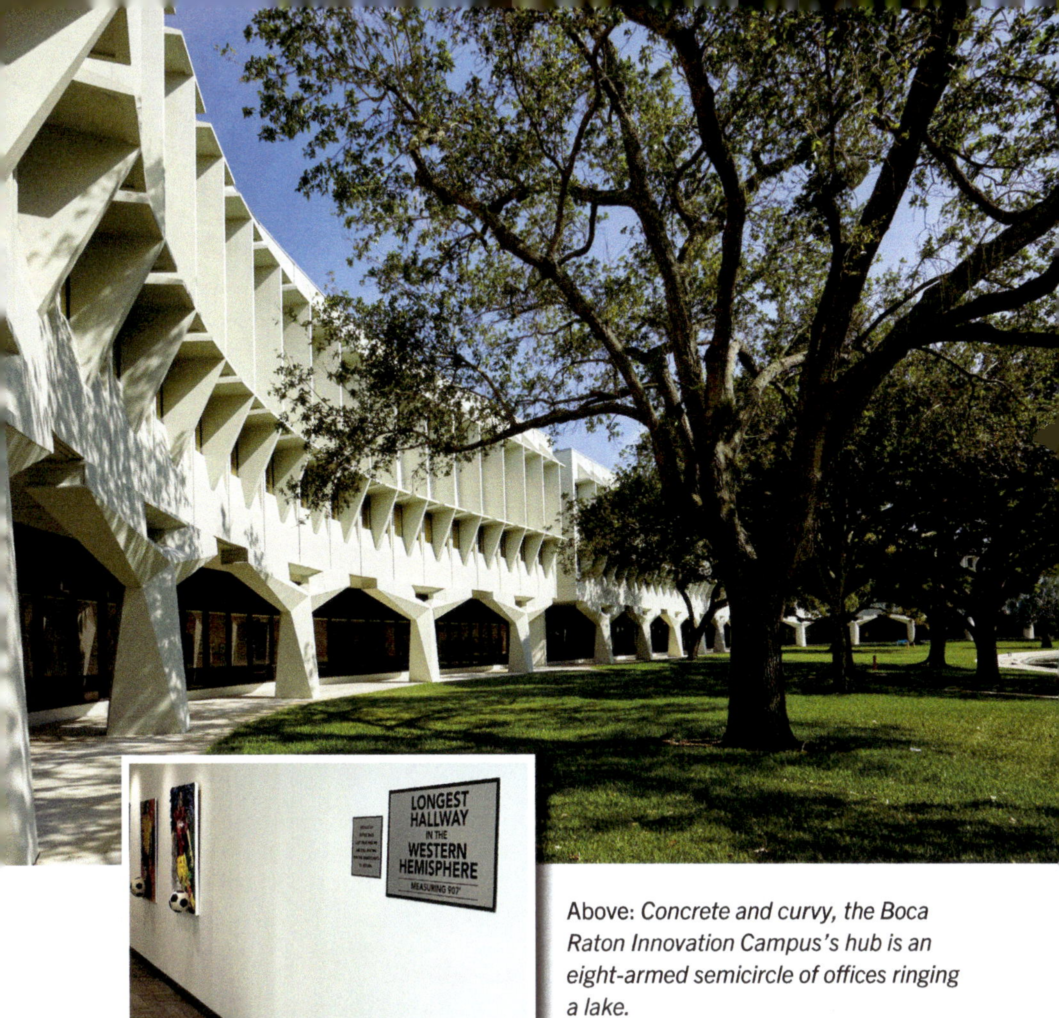

Above: *Concrete and curvy, the Boca Raton Innovation Campus's hub is an eight-armed semicircle of offices ringing a lake.*

Left: *The longest hallway in the western hemisphere is three times the height of the Statue of Liberty. Photos courtesy of CP Group.*

Marcel Brewer's coffee shop at the Boca Raton Innovation Campus has a quintessential photograph of Marcel Breuer on the wall and his signature Cesca chairs at every table.

BOLD FORM

Where is the tallest work of art in the county?

Boynton Beach brought six steel abstracts to its streets in 2017 for a large-scale exhibition by Albert Paley, an exploratory sculptor whose pieces stir intellectual emotions. "Albert on the Avenue" was on display for one year—the artist attended the dedication ceremony—and involved trucking 17 tons of metal to Florida from New York and installing each colossus with a crane. City Hall on East Boynton Beach Boulevard had *Envious Composure*. East Ocean Boulevard was dotted with *Cavalcade*, *Coalescence*, *Moment*, and *Proscenium*. *Stance* was anchored in Dewey Park on Northeast Fourth Street. Each of them was disassembled and returned with the exception of *Cavalcade*. It was purchased by the 500 Ocean residential development as part of the city's public-art program. Valued at $300,000, the 40-foot attraction on the corner of South Federal Highway draws attention from all directions. Its yellow spires, representative of palm fronds, seem to float, and its interlaced purple shapes suggest a sense of sway. Blue, green, orange, and red elements

CAVALCADE

WHAT: Polychromatic splays of steel stretching toward the sky

WHERE: 500 E Ocean Ave., Boynton Beach

COST: Free to view

PRO TIP: Any time of day or night is suitable for catching *Cavalcade* as it is shining either in the sunlight or in the spotlight.

Albert Paley attended Temple University in Philadelphia, earning both bachelor's and master's degrees in fine arts, and started his career as a goldsmith and a jeweler.

Cavalcade *dominates the scenery at an upscale apartment complex. Photo courtesy of city of Boynton Beach*

add to the tropical nature. Paley earned world renown in 1974 when he won a competition at the Smithsonian American Art Museum's Renwick Gallery in Washington, DC. The gallery invited him and more than two dozen other artists to create a set of doors for the gift shop. Paley beat them all with *Portal Gates*.

HANDSOME AND HIRSUTE

How did the hometown hero get his big break?

The starting halfback for the Florida State University Seminoles injured his knee in the second game of his sophomore year. Surgery sidelined him. A few months after the operation, the Palm Beach High School graduate crashed his father's car into a flatbed truck and lost his spleen. His football career ended, and his acting career—a profession he never saw coming—started. Burt Reynolds was 18 when he left Tallahassee and moved back to Riviera Beach. He enrolled in Palm Beach State College in Lake Park to study criminal justice and become a parole officer. While taking an English literature course taught by the college's theater director, he caught a spark. The professor, Watson B. Duncan, whom Reynolds described in his memoir as his greatest mentor, sensed his student's talent and convinced him to audition for a

BURT REYNOLDS

WHAT: A stage graced by the much-missed movie star

WHERE: The Mirror Ballroom is on the second floor of Lake Park Town Hall at 535 Park Ave.

COST: Free to visit

PRO TIP: Palm Beach State College's north campus, now at 3160 PGA Blvd. in Palm Beach Gardens, has two buildings named after Burt Reynolds.

Burt Reynolds produced the television series *B.L. Stryker* from 1989 to 1990, shooting it in Palm Beach County and portraying the houseboat-dwelling Buddy Lee Stryker.

Above: *The Mirror Ballroom has a pecky-cypress ceiling, from which a working mirror ball spins, and a beautifully restored oak floor. Photo courtesy of town of Lake Park*

Left: *Burt Reynolds shows off his speed and his moves at Florida State University. Photo from Florida Memory*

play in the Mirror Ballroom. Reynolds's performance in *Outward Bound* earned him a Florida State Drama Award and a scholarship to the Hyde Park Playhouse in New York. His four-decade run included more than 100 films, notably 1972's critically acclaimed *Deliverance* and 1977's cult classic *Smokey and the Bandit*. Before either was released, the man with the mustache became a household name when he posed nude for *Cosmopolitan* magazine in an infamous issue that sold 1.5 million copies.

MAKING THE CUT

Why are five municipal courses in the county part of the Florida Historic Golf Trail?

The North Palm Beach Country Club, which was called the Palm Beach Winter Club when architect Seth Raynor designed it in 1926, has an intriguing past. In 1935, the club was acquired by Harry Oakes, the British baronet who would later be bludgeoned and burned in the Bahamas. Oakes, at one point among the richest men in America, lived in the stately building on a part-time basis. His brutal murder remains unsolved more than 80 years after prime suspect Marie Alfred de Fonquereaux de Marigny, the French count who married Oakes's daughter, was acquitted. Notwithstanding the sensational trial and its ties to North Palm Beach, the country club is on the list because of its trademarked Jack Nicklaus Signature links. The Lake Worth Beach Golf Club, also established in 1926, fronts the Intracoastal Waterway and offers a scenic place to take a swing. The Delray Beach Golf Club was laid out by architect Donald Ross, and in 1966, it welcomed the Louise Suggs Delray Beach Invitational, a tournament named for one of the founders of the LPGA. The Boca Raton is a championship-level amenity at a five-star resort. The Park

ABOVE PAR

WHAT: Tees, fairways, and greens that shaped golf's heritage

WHERE: North Palm Beach Country Club, 951 US Hwy. 1; the Park, 7301 Georgia Ave., West Palm Beach; Lake Worth Beach Golf Club, One Seventh Ave. N; Delray Beach Golf Club, 2200 Highland Ave.; the Boca Raton, 501 E Camino Real

COST: Fees vary depending on the time of year.

PRO TIP: Jack Nicklaus, arguably the greatest golfer of all time, is a longtime North Palm Beach resident.

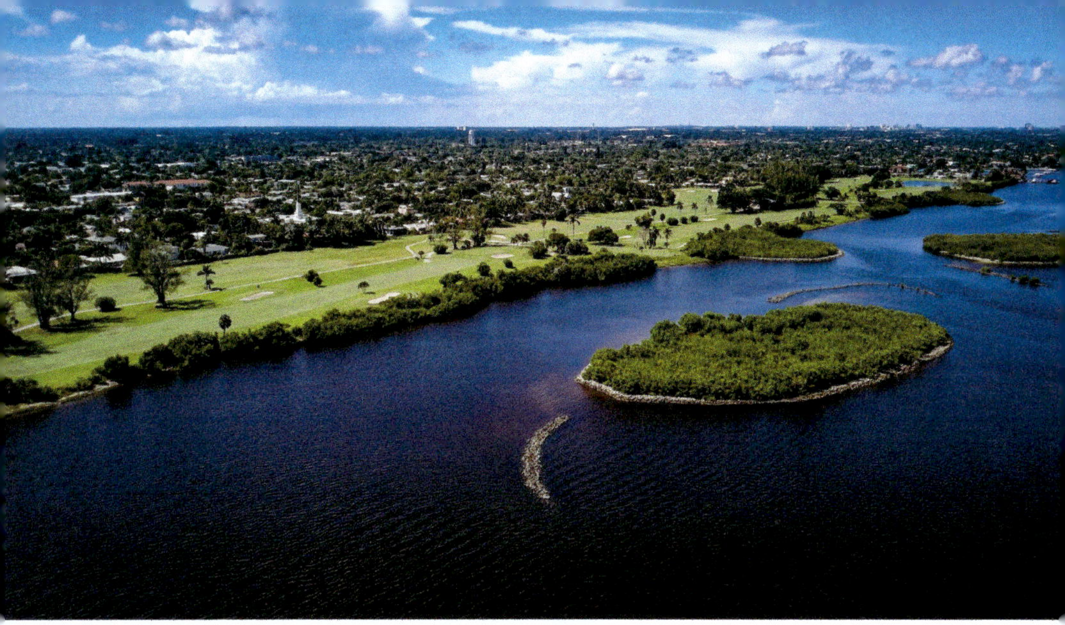

Above: *The Lake Worth Beach Golf Club has a series of skill-testing doglegs. Photo courtesy of city of Lake Worth Beach*

Left: *The North Palm Beach Country Club challenges golfers of all levels. Photo courtesy of North Palm Beach Country Club*

in West Palm Beach is the newest addition to the Florida Historic Golf Trail. It is operated in partnership with the city and has a goal of bringing more youths into the game.

The Florida Historic Golf Trail, a project by the Florida Department of State's Division of Historical Resources, identifies publicly playable venues of significance.

IT'S SHOWTIME!

Why do ghost stories continue to emerge from the downtown theater?

The area's most historic stage celebrated its centennial in 2024 and, like other stages of yesteryear throughout the country and the world, it silently seethes with paranormal activity. As many as five apparitions are said to haunt the place. The most loyal is Lucien Oakley, who with his brother Clarence Oakley built the Art Deco Lake Worth Playhouse, then called the Oakley Theatre. Opening night thrilled the crowd with an orchestra and an organist providing accompaniment to scenes from the 1920 Broadway play *Welcome Stranger*. The decade ended with the hurricane of 1928 and the stock-market crash of 1929 shuttering the siblings' show-business dreams. A despondent Lucien Oakley committed suicide in 1931. A penniless Clarence Oakley suffered a fatal heart attack one year later. Since their deaths, reports of strange occurrences have accumulated. Actors describe unexplained taps on their shoulders while performing solo. Crew members cite

LAKE WORTH PLAYHOUSE

WHAT: A 296-seat venue that cannot seem to shake its spooks

WHERE: 713 Lake Ave., Lake Worth Beach

COST: Ticket prices vary.

PRO TIP: In March, the Lake Worth Playhouse presents the campy Swede Fest Palm Beach, and its equally haunted black-box studio presents the indie L-Dub Film Festival.

Lucien Oakley is buried in his home state of Illinois, and Clarence Oakley is buried in an unmarked grave in Lake Worth Beach's Pinecrest Cemetery.

Top: *The Art Deco Society of Palm Beach County, a nonprofit promoting awareness of the 20th-century design form, indexed the Lake Worth Playhouse as the oldest building on its register.*

Left: *Clarence Oakley. Photo courtesy of Lake Worth Playhouse*

Right: *Lucian Oakley. Photo courtesy of Lake Worth Playhouse*

finding items mysteriously moved around. Handprints suddenly appear on the walls. Sometimes the ghost light flickers when it is unplugged. The disclosures prompted a visit to the Lake Worth Playhouse by a team of electronically outfitted enthusiasts who track paranormal activity. They detected energy shifts within its spaces and concluded that low- and high-vibrational spirits exist.

FICTITIOUS NAME

To what extent did the US government lie about a toxic testing site in the swamp?

The make-believe town on 9,000 acres of land in western Palm Beach County had two large factories that supposedly manufactured fertilizer. They did not. The crude buildings, slanted sheds, test stands, and underground pipelines of Apix, population zero, harbored a new type of fuel for planes and rockets during the height of the Cold War. Called "Project Suntan," the ruse was orchestrated by the Air Force, the Florida Game and Fresh Water Fish Commission (now the Florida Fish and Wildlife Conservation Commission), and prominent aerospace company Pratt & Whitney. In 1956, the parties colluded to obtain a piece of property in a remote location—they chose one next to a wildlife refuge—and name it Apix, an acronym for Air Products Incorporated, Experimental. Apix was platted on paper as a community of small homes to throw speculators off the scent. The first phase of the project, "Mama Bear," cost more than $6 million and aimed to liquefy half a

An aerial view of "Project Suntan" shows its harsh environs. Photos from Florida Memory

Engines undergo tests in Apix.

APIX

WHAT: The site of a cloak-and-dagger operation that eventually failed

WHERE: Beeline Hwy. near Indiantown Rd.

COST: Free to explore

PRO TIP: Beware of alligators.

ton of hydrogen daily. The second phase of the project, "Papa Bear," had a $27 million price tag and a 30-ton-a-day goal. With improved propulsion from liquid hydrogen, American aircrafts would one-up those belonging to the Soviets. Citing cost concerns and feasibility issues, officials canceled "Project Suntan" in 1959. Apix was erased from the map.

Curiously, East and West Apix Circles connect to East and West Whitney Drives in the middle of a bona fide residential area in Jupiter.

LARGER THAN LIFE

Where did the influential environmental stalwart grow up?

Born in 1933 in New York City to Joseph and Permelia Reed, the middle child who would become US assistant secretary of the interior spent the majority of his life in Jupiter Island. His parents first visited the mostly untouched barrier east of Hobe Sound two years before he was born and immediately purchased a lot for a winter home. The Reeds formed a land company and ended up acquiring 2,000 additional acres. Every January, the family made the move to South Florida from Greenwich, Connecticut. They built sandcastles on the beach, trolled for fish in the Loxahatchee River, and hiked around the citrus-tree-dotted grounds. Nathaniel P. Reed wrote in his memoir that he had fallen in love with the area and, for that reason, made it his permanent residence in 1959. He joined his parents in managing the land company and the Jupiter

NATHANIEL P. REED

WHAT: A 1,091-acre network managed by the US Fish & Wildlife Service that is named for the tireless advocate

WHERE: The Nathaniel P. Reed Hobe Sound National Wildlife Refuge is at 13640 SE Federal Hwy.

COST: Fee for admission

PRO TIP: The United States would be without the 1972 Clean Water Act and the 1973 Endangered Species Act had it not been for the efforts of Nathaniel P. Reed.

While inspecting the greens at the Jupiter Island Club, the six-foot, one-inch outdoorsman heard a commotion on the fourth hole and brazenly rescued a dog from an alligator's jaws.

Nathaniel P. Reed poses for a portrait at his home in Jupiter Island. Photo by Madeline Gray/USA Today Network via Imagn Images

Island Club and carried out their mission of a harmonious development in an extraordinary setting that did not deserve big condominiums. Reed served as an adviser to Florida Gov. Claude Kirk and was appointed to the cabinet during the Nixon and Ford administrations. He never took a salary. The gentle giant died in 2018 at age 84 after hitting his head on a rock during a fishing expedition in Canada.

CASA APAVA

What piece of the landmark estate was relocated to Pan's Garden?

A large slab of coquina accented with blue and yellow tiles and Spanish mosaics all revealing their age brings a touch of sentiment to Pan's Garden. The timeless architectural element that came to rest amid thousands of native plants belonged to Casa Apava, a revered residence on the south end of the island. Abram Garfield, the youngest son of President James Garfield, sketched the original floor plan for Chester and Frances Bolton. Chester Bolton was a wealthy Ohio congressman, and Frances Bolton was a Standard Oil heiress. Their vast riches enabled them to build the dreamiest of mansions. Casa Apava was opulent. Occupying 17 acres, it had 26 rooms and nine fireplaces. At the heart of the home was a 160-foot-long series of meandering living spaces designed to capture ocean and bay breezes. Its showstopper was a four-story belvedere-topped tower with Mediterranean flair. The Garden Club of Palm Beach featured the property on a house tour in 1959. In 1993, when plans were announced

NOBLE FOUNTAIN

WHAT: A half-acre green space with a hunk of history

WHERE: 386 Hibiscus Ave.

COST: Free to explore

PRO TIP: Pan's Garden is named after the Frederick MacMonnies bronze *Pan of Rohallion*, the god of shepherds who guards the flock.

Casa Apava, at 1300 S Ocean Blvd., was completed in 1919 and recognized by the Palm Beach Landmarks Preservation Commission in 1980.

Casa Apava sold for $71.2 million in 2015. Photo from Library of Congress

to subdivide the land (the new owner's financing fell through, and the parcels were never separated), the Preservation Foundation of Palm Beach relocated the Casa Apava wall. Disassembled into several massive sections, it was reassembled in Pan's Garden as part of a water feature.

TOES IN THE SAND

How many miles did the shoeless workers walk?

"Neither snow nor rain nor heat nor gloom of night stays these couriers from the swift completion of their appointed rounds." The unofficial motto of the US Postal Service would read a bit better in South Florida if it stated, "Neither rain nor heat nor humidity nor alligators nor sharks nor gloom of night stays these barefoot mailmen from the swift completion of their appointed rounds." The term "barefoot mailmen" traces its roots to novelist Theodore Pratt, who wrote a book about the challenging and dangerous Star Route the public servants traversed. Established in 1885, the Star Route stretched 60 miles from Hypoluxo to Miami, all of it on the beach. The men found that slogging along the shoreline barefoot was easier, and doing so became a best practice. The trip took six days—three down and three back—dramatically shortening delivery times. Prior to the Star Route, a parcel sent from the east coast had to go to Jacksonville, Cedar Key, and Key West in order to reach Miami

BAREFOOT MAILMEN

WHAT: A remembrance of the letter carriers of lore

WHERE: Hypoluxo Scrub Natural Area is at 150 Hypoluxo Rd.

COST: Free to explore

PRO TIP: The Barefoot Mailman Inn & Suites in Lantana is named for the intrepid employees who provided a line of communication where there had been none before.

West Palm Beach lawyer Harvey Oyer, the great-grandnephew of a barefoot mailman, has written a series of children's books about his great-granduncle titled the *Adventures of Charlie Pierce*.

The names of some of the barefoot mailmen appear on a plaque at the base of a bronze in the Hypoluxo Scrub Natural Area. Photo courtesy of Palm Beach Pack & Paddle Club

as the infrastructure was not yet in place. The barefoot mailmen braved the elements for seven years, and during that time, one lost his life. A 14-foot statue honoring the courageous souls of the past can be admired at the Hypoluxo Scrub Natural Area.

MEDS AND MALTS

What keeps customers coming to the streetside staple?

The old-Americana atmosphere of a cozy diner with reasonably priced comfort food and a soda jerk behind the Formica counter has largely vanished. Green's Pharmacy, sporting a black-and-white-checkered linoleum floor, a row of spiffy barstools, and nostalgic signs throughout, is an exception. Established in 1938, the eatery is a reminder of simpler times. Friendly folks congregate at breakfast to sip coffee, dig into an omelet, and talk shop. Those who come in for a midday meal will find restaurant rarities like liverwurst sandwiches, sardine platters, and a tuna-salad-stuffed tomato surprise on the menu. Most guests do not know what an egg cream is (the classic New York recipe calls for milk, chocolate-flavored syrup, and seltzer) yet end up ordering it anyway. Green's Pharmacy has all of that and more plus daily specials written on the chalkboard. Across from the 82-seat luncheonette is the other half of the operation—a well-stocked drugstore with aisles of products.

GREEN'S PHARMACY

WHAT: A days-of-old destination

WHERE: 151 N County Rd.

COST: Free to visit

PRO TIP: Green's Pharmacy is one block away from the beach and carries everything from sunscreen to sunglasses to frozen desserts on a stick.

President John F. Kennedy frequently ducked beneath the striped awnings of Green's Pharmacy—it was two-and-a-half miles south of the Winter White House—for a milkshake.

Green's Pharmacy is a one-stop shop.

Patrons can fill prescriptions while they wait and use a house account to do so. The pharmacy is not entirely retro; it accepts electronic prescriptions, too. The nearly 90-year-old business and its turn-back-the-clock milieu is open every day of the year. The pharmacy is closed Sundays.

HANGING WITH THE KENNEDYS

Why do patrons pay big bucks to enter the small bar?

For one brief shining moment, President John F. Kennedy had his Winter White House in Palm Beach. The estate on North Ocean Boulevard did more than provide an escape from the up-north cold. JFK wrote his inaugural address (of "ask not what your country can do for you—ask what you can do for your country" fame) at the Mediterranean-style mansion. He also penned part of his Pulitzer Prize–winning book *Profiles in Courage* there. The imprint made on the island by the gone-too-soon hero of democracy endures inside a 3,500-square-foot bar in downtown West Palm Beach. Camelot embraces the family-oriented, fun-loving ways of the 35th president, whose 1,036 days in office will forever be associated with the Broadway musical about King Arthur, Queen Guenevere, and the Knights of the Round Table. The nautical nightclub has whitewashed walls, wood paneling, and plenty of maritime decor such as old anchors and ship's

CAMELOT

WHAT: A semiprivate club for the sophisticated set

WHERE: 114 S Narcissus Ave., West Palm Beach

COST: Cover charge to enter

PRO TIP: Memberships are available that include half-price drinks plus other party perks.

Camelot sits in the same spot as the long-lost Kandy Bar that entertained many a male pleasure-seeker when it offered live burlesque.

Above: *"Don't let it be forgot . . . once there was a spot . . . known as Camelot."*

Left: *Hail to the chief! Photo from Wikimedia Commons*

lights. The DJ booth pulsates behind the windshield of a boat. Framed pictures are everywhere, including one of "Jack" enjoying an ice-cream cone on his yacht. Camelot and its dance floor are open to the public from 9 p.m. to 3 a.m. Wednesdays, Fridays, and Saturdays. Beer, wine, and craft cocktails also are served on the outside patio.

KILLING FIELD

What unspeakable acts occurred beneath the ancient oak?

Murder. Mutilation. Rape. All with a sadistic twist. In 1977, the headless remains of two young women surfaced near a knotty trunk in an old-growth area of Port St. Lucie. They belonged to Colette Goodenough and Barbara Ann Wilcox, both 19, who were last seen in 1973 hitchhiking to Florida from Iowa. The women were abducted, brought to the remote location, tortured, and as rotting rope and a noose would attest, hanged. Further investigation revealed the offender returned to the scene on multiple occasions to pillage the bodies, eventually scattering what was left in the dirt. A psychological profile of the man believed to be responsible for the reign of terror points to a deep-seeded narcissist with a complete disregard for human life and a capability for profound cruelty. Since then, the Devil Tree has been an eerie draw in Oak Hammock Park. Hooded figures lurking in the thicket and wailing sounds emanating from the distance have been reported as have sightings of occult worshippers

DEVIL TREE

WHAT: A forest denizen that dates back 150 years

WHERE: 1982 SW Villanova Rd., Port St. Lucie

COST: Free to explore

PRO TIP: Local author Keith Rommel retells the tale of the wooded beast in a novel titled the *Devil Tree.*

While the hitchhikers' case has gone cold, it has been linked to Gerard Schaefer, a deranged Martin County Sheriff's Office deputy convicted in two similarly gruesome deaths.

The Devil Tree has a sinister silhouette.

gathering after dark. Attempts to cut down the Devil Tree have failed. In one instance, the teeth of a crosscut saw were sheared off. In another, an axe rebounded from the impenetrable bark and split open the head of the lumberjack.

LIONS AND TAPIRS AND BLUE-TONGUED SKINKS, OH MY!

How did Loxahatchee land the first cageless zoo in the country?

A group of overseas entrepreneurs envisioned an outdoor attraction that would bring the fauna of Africa to the United States. They wanted to give Americans the opportunity to encounter exotic species from the continent without the expense of traveling there. Loxahatchee, in unincorporated western Palm Beach County, was selected as the site of the drive-through park because of its ideal climate and undeveloped expanse. Lion Country Safari opened in 1967 to a crowd of summer visitors in awe of the free-roaming kings of the jungle surrounding their vehicles. It ushered in a new era in zoology. *USA Today* named it one of the 10 best safari parks in the country, and Fodor's Travel's USA Travel Guide ranked it among the top three. For a nominal fee, guests can steer their way through 300-plus acres of forests, plains, prairies,

LION COUNTRY SAFARI

WHAT: A four-mile tour filled with wild things

WHERE: 2003 Lion Country Safari Rd.

COST: Ticket prices vary.

PRO TIP: The critters tend to be more out and about in wet weather, making rainy days the best time to observe them.

Other things to do at Lion Country Safari include the Flamingo Mingle Experience, giraffe feeding, paddleboat rides, and a walk-through adventure area.

Above: *Giraffe crossing is commonplace. Photo courtesy of Lion Country Safari*

Left: *Lion Country Safari draws 500,000 tourists annually.*

savannas, and other habitats similar to those found in Mozambique, Tanzania, and Zimbabwe. The paved circuit is home to nearly 800 mammals and reptiles representing not only Africa but also Asia, Australia, Europe, North America, and South America. Accredited by the Association of Zoos & Aquariums, Lion Country Safari maintains the largest herd of zebras in the United States and has seen more than 40 rhinoceros calves come into the world.

BRAVE AND BROAD-CHESTED

Who did the Croatian-born South Florida actor play in the movies?

He saves the daughter of an Amazon queen from insurgents searching for hidden treasure in *Tarzan in the Golden Grotto*. In *Tarzan and the Rainbow*, he protects a dead monarch's son from a mercenary who wants to take over as king of a Chilean village. Steve Sipek, the loincloth-wearing, vine-swinging portrayer of the hero, starred in both Spanish-language titles, *Tarzán en la Gruta del Oro* in 1969 and *Tarzán y el Arco Iris* in 1972. As a boy, Stjepan Šipek watched Johnny Weissmuller play the role and dreamed of embodying the character. He learned the machinist's trade in his home country prior to moving to Canada where he trained as a swimmer and a wrestler. By the time the tall, sculpted 22-year-old with the dark shock of hair made his way to Miami, he had garnered the attention of producers. During the filming of *Tarzan and the Rainbow*, Sipek, whose stage name was Steve Hawkes, suffered severe

STEVE SIPEK

WHAT: A compound that was owned by a real-life "Ape Man"

WHERE: 3384 C Rd., Loxahatchee

COST: Not for sale

PRO TIP: A recent appraisal valued the five-acre compound at $660,540.

One of the tigers at Steve Sipek's sanctuary escaped in 2004, and the ensuing manhunt ended with the animal being fatally shot by a wildlife official.

Steve Sipek stood six feet, one inch tall and weighed 228 pounds. Photo courtesy of Digital Homeland

burns while tied to a tree. A lion dragged him from the flames in a miraculous rescue. The injury ended his career, and he spent the rest of his life advocating for big cats. He founded a sanctuary in Loxahatchee and housed not only the lion that saved him but also cougars, leopards, panthers, and tigers for 30 years until his death in 2019 at age 77.

WOW FACTOR

What makes the secluded beach the best spot to see the motion of the ocean?

The natural phenomenon that occurs on a barrier island in Hobe Sound is as dazzling as it is dumbfounding. At any given moment, a geyser of frothy saltwater will shoot skyward, traveling up to 50 feet in the air before splashing down on the dramatically shaped Anastasia limestone outcropping. The action resembles that of hot lava spewing from an erupting volcano. Carved for centuries by the sea and the wind, the sedimentary rock comprised of coral fragments, shell pieces, and small fossils has a network of gaps, shelves, and tunnels that momentarily trap waves before forcefully redirecting them into vertical streams. Cell phones are a must for capturing

A shady seagrape path leads to the shore at Blowing Rocks Preserve. Photos by Mike Olliver

---

Blowing Rocks Preserve is open daily with the exception of major holidays, and an optional per-guest donation goes toward maintaining the native coastal habitat.

Blowing Rocks Preserve does its thing.

BLOWING ROCKS PRESERVE

WHAT: A jaw-dropping display along an unspoiled shoreline

WHERE: 574 S Beach Rd., Hobe Sound

COST: Free to explore

PRO TIP: Blowing Rocks Preserve puts on its best show during high tide in moderate to rough offshore conditions.

photos and videos of the dynamic events unfolding in and around the jagged structure. Managed by the Nature Conservancy's Center for Conservation Initiatives, a program that encourages land stewardship, Blowing Rocks Preserve also features several short trails that crisscross the area, a boardwalk that rambles through a mangrove forest, and a scenic loop around a pollinator garden. A Beach Bucket Foundation station provides an opportunity for visitors to help protect the environment by collecting trash. Those interested in contributing on a scientific level can download the iNaturalist app and submit images of plants and animals observed within the 73-acre sanctuary.

SUBMERGED SCENERY

What unusual objects form the biodiverse aquatic attraction?

Concrete modules shaped like hammerhead sharks lurk beneath the surface to the west. To the east, a couple of boat wrecks and some scaffolding shelter swimming creatures that dart in and out of nooks and crannies. In the middle, shopping carts resting on the sandy bottom simulate living coral. The junk plopped along 800 feet of beach in the shadow of the Blue Heron Bridge makes up the Phil Foster Memorial Park Snorkel Trail. Around each pile, there is beauty to behold. Those geared up with masks and fins will see angelfish, drums, grunts, flounder, jacks, sheepshead, and tarpon in addition to octopus, rays, and seahorses flourishing in the artificial habitat that *Sport Diver Magazine* named one of the 50 best dive destinations in the world. Both novice and skilled snorkelers can find their comfort zones as the trail's depth ranges from an easy five feet to a more challenging 15 feet. While exploring, it is important to follow a few rules to preserve the trail and

PHIL FOSTER MEMORIAL PARK SNORKEL TRAIL

WHAT: A route of repurposed debris harboring underwater denizens

WHERE: 900 E Blue Heron Blvd., Riviera Beach

COST: Free to explore

PRO TIP: The optimal time to check out the Phil Foster Memorial Park Snorkel Trail is 30 minutes prior to high tide.

The Phil Foster Memorial Park Snorkel Trail is home to an assortment of exquisite species, including flying gurnards, nudibranchs, sea robins, and stargazers, rarely found elsewhere.

Top: *The Phil Foster Memorial Park Snorkel Trail encompasses 15 acres.*

Bottom: *A Reef Smart sign has helpful information.*

its precious marine life. Do not step on or touch the structures, and, in accordance with Florida Fish and Wildlife Conservation Commission regulations, do not feed the schools or harvest any organisms from the area.

FERMENTING AND FLEECING

How did the homeopathic huckster succeed in swindling wealthy northerners?

As a teenager, James Munyon experimented with herbs and roots as therapeutic remedies. His bottled his formulations and sold them door to door. As an adult, the slick man in the suit with the gift of gab and a knack for marketing started a company and touted his product as a cure-all for rheumatism, nervousness, sleeplessness, stress, and other ailments. He named it Munyon's Paw-Paw. The primary distribution point was the Hygeia Hotel, named for the Greek goddess of

The Hygeia Hotel had 21 rooms overlooking a wide lagoon. Photo from Digital Commons at University of South Florida/ Hampton Dunn Collection of Florida Postcards

---

James Munyon undoubtedly is having the last laugh with the reintroduction of his once-bogus elixir by a local craft distillery that is offering it as a premium Florida liqueur.

James Munyon was born in 1848 in Connecticut.

JAMES MUNYON

WHAT: An interpretive site for South Florida's first snake-oil salesman

WHERE: John D. MacArthur Beach State Park is at 10900 Jack Nicklaus Dr. in North Palm Beach

COST: Fee for admission

PRO TIP: John D. MacArthur Beach State Park has 436 acres of natural habitat, 1.6 miles of undeveloped beach, and a 1,600-foot boardwalk bridging a teeming estuary.

health, on an island he acquired in northern Palm Beach County. He peddled the potion to well-to-do visitors who, thanks to an advertising blitz that included a song titled "Down Where the Paw-Paw Grows," journeyed south to get their hands on it. Little did they know they were buying a simple mixture of papaya juice and sulfur water. The Hygeia Hotel burned down in 1917, and Munyon died one year later at age 69. Traces of its foundation can be found in the thick brush on the south end of the island that now is part of John D. MacArthur Beach State Park. Accessible by boat, it is largely a mangrove habitat with nature trails and picnic pavilions.

BELLY UP

How did the beer-pouring, booze-flowing business get its name?

Ralph Crooks, who at the time was the chief of Jupiter's volunteer fire department, owned a rustic waterfront lodge that served hamburgers and hush puppies to the men on shift. Called Ralph's Fishing Camp, it was the predecessor of Ralph's Stand Up Bar. The camp operated north of where Alternate A1A crosses the Loxahatchee River via the R.E. "Pete" Damon Memorial Bridge. (Damon, a former town commissioner and clerk, tended the span for two decades.) Crooks eventually moved his operation to Center Street, and in 1948, Ralph's Stand Up Bar was on the map. Patrons downing drinks at its wooden, waist-high counter do not sit on stools. Rather, they rest a foot on the metal rail that runs along the base of the floor. Reminiscent of an old Western saloon, minus the spittoons, the lovable dive has plenty of whiskey to go around. Out front, dramatic cutout silhouettes of a boot- and hat-wearing cowboy and a busty woman in high heels frame the entrance. Out back, a cozy patio provides

RALPH'S STAND UP BAR

WHAT: An in-the-know gathering place

WHERE: 113 Center St., Jupiter

COST: Comparably cheap drinks

PRO TIP: Things are old-school at Ralph's Stand Up Bar—it accepts cash only, and food is not offered.

The easily missed hole-in-the-wall has a daily happy hour, organizes regular motorcycle nights, plans themed holiday events, and supports the community through charity drives.

Above: *Ralph's Stand Up Bar starts serving at noon seven days a week.*

Left: *Ralph's Stand Up Bar has a laid-back atmosphere and lots of history.*

a shady spot to hang in the balmy South Florida weather. Live music from local bands rocks the room on weekends. Crooks died 22 years after opening the doors to the oldest licensed alcoholic-beverage establishment in Palm Beach County.

CRUCIAL WATERSHED

What federally designated title does seven-and-a-half miles of the blueway boast?

Shaded by moss-draped cypress trees whose coniferous needles give a tea-color glow to the water, the "Wild and Scenic" Loxahatchee River lives up to its description. The earthy smell of decomposing leaves below the surface and the exhilarating sight of a great blue heron skulking through them in search of prey prove it. Anyone paddling through the Loxahatchee will agree it is an amazing antidote to the brick-and-mortar world. Only the sounds of nature can be heard—a splash here and a trickle there, echoing bird calls from above, the rustle of scampering critters. Canoers and kayakers will encounter lazy alligators sunning on the banks, playful otters slipping in and out of view, and motionless turtles clinging to logs. The Loxahatchee, specifically the northwest fork, is protected by the Wild and Scenic Rivers Act of 1968. The legislation recognizes "outstandingly remarkable scenic, recreational, geologic, fish and wildlife, historic, cultural, or other similar values" and mandates their protection "for the benefit and enjoyment of present and future generations." Of the northwest fork's seven-and-a-half miles, an approximate one and a half are "Wild," and an approximate five and a half

LOXAHATCHEE RIVER

WHAT: A peaceful, slow-flowing subtropical system

WHERE: The headwaters are in Riverbend Park in Jupiter, and the mouth is in Jonathan Dickinson State Park in Hobe Sound.

COST: Riverbend Park is free to explore, and there is a fee for admission to Jonathan Dickinson State Park.

PRO TIP: The seven-and-a-half miles are full of surprises, including two dams that require portage and the vestiges of a camp that belonged to a man who lived off the land.

Cypress knees, part of the cypress tree's root system, give a mystical touch to the swampy environs.

are "Scenic." The remainder is recreational. The Loxahatchee has two other forks that make up its 200-plus-square-mile basin—the north fork and the southwest fork, both of which are surrounded by residential development.

The Loxahatcheee River is one of two "Wild and Scenic" rivers in Florida, the other being the Wekiva River north of Orlando.

WISE GUY

Why did Al Capone own property on a tomato field in Jupiter?

The notorious Chicago mob boss clandestinely purchased a home and 180 acres of agricultural land surrounding it during the Prohibition Era, his heyday. He was running a bootlegging racket in addition to gambling and prostitution rings in the Windy City and needed a far-away, off-the-grid hideout for his associates. The tomato field in Jupiter off of what then was called Italian Farms Road did the trick. The home served as a safe haven for Al Capone's goons and is said to have kept some of them alive and well. While the OG did not live on the property and was never seen in its vicinity, there are reports attributed to longtime residents that

SCARFACE

WHAT: A Mafia man's stash house

WHERE: 16133 Jupiter Farms Rd.

COST: Free to visit

PRO TIP: The owner of the Town & Country Feed & Supply store is Ritchey Brown, Burt Reynolds's great-nephew.

Al Capone mugs for the camera after a 1930 arrest. Photos from Wikimedia Commons

Burt Reynolds wore a red Trans Am jacket in Smokey and the Bandit II.

gangsters were observed driving in and out. Fast-forward to the 1960s, and the plot thickens. The property, after exchanging hands a couple of times, eventually became Burt Reynolds Ranch, the beloved actor's abode. Reynolds had title to it for several decades and operated a petting zoo that families adored. He filmed scenes from *Smokey and the Bandit II* there in 1980, and in 1988, he married Loni Anderson in the development's small chapel. The Town & Country Feed & Supply store on present-day Jupiter Farms Road now stands in the original structure's place.

Al Capone had another connection to South Florida—Miami—where he lived on and off in a Palm Island villa until his death in 1947 at age 48.

LIVING ARCHIVE

Where did two gruesome US offenses against an Indigenous tribe occur?

Loxahatchee River Battlefield Park, a 60-acre swath of land maintained by Palm Beach County, saw a lot of action during the Second Seminole War. A pair of significant fights erupted in January of 1838, nine days apart, during the US campaign to remove Native Americans east of the Mississippi River. The first Battle of the Loxahatchee occurred January 15, when Lt. Levin Powell led 100 soldiers in small boats through the southwest fork of the Loxahatchee River. The Seminoles overpowered the soldiers using musket fire and forced a retreat. The second Battle of the Loxahatchee occurred January 24, when Maj. Gen. Thomas Jesup led 1,600 soldiers on foot and on horse to the headwaters. The Seminoles managed to hold off the soldiers while hundreds of noncombatants reached safety. Both battles begat the Third Seminole War, a series of skirmishes from 1855 to 1858 that concluded the US campaign. A truce was called,

SECOND SEMINOLE WAR

WHAT: A park with a past

WHERE: 9060 W Indiantown Rd., Jupiter

COST: Free to explore

PRO TIP: Loxahatchee River Battlefield Park shares an entrance with Riverbend Park and is in the northwest quadrant of the grounds.

The Loxahatchee Battlefield Preservationists, a volunteer group dedicated to telling the story of the Seminoles, brings the Trail of Tears to life during an annual two-day reenactment.

Top: *A memorial stone and a wood fence guard the Tree of Tears.*

Bottom: *Park hours are sunrise to sunset seven days a week. Photos courtesy of Loxahatchee Battle Preservationists*

yet a treaty was rejected, and in an act of betrayal under a white flag, nearly 700 Seminoles were captured and forced to walk the Trail of Tears. Anchoring Loxahatchee River Battlefield Park is an ancient oak referred to as the Tree of Tears that signifies the pain and suffering of the agonizing journey.

MAKING A SPLASH

Who are the 1960s-era beach bums promoting the pop-up gallery?

Corky Roche religiously paddled out to the spot where the 440-foot freighter *Amaryllis* ran aground in 1965 north of the Palm Beach Inlet. Tom Warnke created the Cripple Creek Surf Club in 1966 in Boynton Beach and is an East Coast Surfing Hall of Fame inductee. Fred Salmon started the Sandy Shores Surf Club in 1967 on Singer Island and befriended a local photographer chronicling the exploding surf scene. Together with Bill Keeton, the president of the Jupiter Noseriders Surf Club who died in 2021 at age 68, they founded the Surfing Florida Museum. Since 2008, the museum has had 42 traveling exhibits in venues such as the Cornell Art Museum in Delray Beach, the Elliott Museum in Stuart, and the Richard & Pat Johnson Palm Beach County History Museum in West Palm Beach. While the Lantana Public Library has an ongoing display of items at its surf-themed facility, the museum is in search of a permanent place to preserve an indelible part of Florida culture. After

SURFING FLORIDA MUSEUM

WHAT: A curated collection in search of a new home

WHERE: The Lantana Public Library is at 205 W Ocean Ave.

COST: Free to visit

PRO TIP: The Surfing Florida Museum's annual fundraiser is a golf tournament that supports the nonprofit's mission of sharing the history of the sport.

Stranded by Hurricane Betsy, a Category 4 storm, the *Amaryllis* remained beached for three years and formed an ideal break that became the state's top surfing destination.

Above: *Surfboards dangle from the ceiling at the Lantana Public Library. Photo by Brittany DeJesus*

Left: *The contents of the Surfing Florida Museum include a 1956 Robertson-Sweet foam and fiberglass surfboard christened Lukia.*

having three locations in a span of 10 years, the extensive collection of 100 surfboards, 85 panels, piles of memorabilia, and reels of film, along with thousands of Kodachrome slides, is crammed in a locked storage facility in Lake Park.

ROAD WARRIORS

Where did the improbable African American art movement emerge?

In Fort Pierce, the life of a high-school student attending segregated Lincoln Park Academy changed the day he met an influential local artist. When Alfred Hair, who would become the catalyst for the Florida Highwaymen, was introduced to A.E. "Bean" Backus, the young man's path was set. Hair knew he wanted to be an artist, and he learned from his mentor, a World War II veteran who opened a home studio on Moore's Creek. A promising protégé, Hair took an airy and dreamy approach to his luscious landscapes of old Florida. He also figured out how to earn a profit and support his family. He painted in the backyard of his property with other like-minded creatives who adopted his simple technique while maintaining their individual styles. Because white-owned galleries categorically rejected black-made works for inclusion in exhibits, the band of 25 men and one woman went mobile.

FLORIDA HIGHWAYMEN

WHAT: An institution extolling a group of black artists who brushstroked their way through racial barriers

WHERE: The Florida Highwaymen Museum is at 1234 Ave. D in Fort Pierce.

COST: Fee for admission

PRO TIP: The Florida Highwaymen produced, marketed, and sold a body of work that exceeds 200,000 pieces.

Alfred Hair was an up-and-coming 29-year-old with a wife and four children when he was murdered in 1970 during a barroom brawl.

Above: *The royal poinciana tree was an element in many Florida Highwaymen scenes, including this one by Alfred Hair.*

Left: *Alfred Hair was prolific and sometimes hired sales representatives, loaning them a car so he could keep busy in the shop. Photos courtesy of Doretha Hair Truesdell*

They stacked their still-wet oils on Upson board in the trunks of their cars and sold them along US Highway 1. In honor of the trailblazers, the Fort Pierce Redevelopment Agency has transformed a 3,200-square-foot building in the middle of the Highwaymen Heritage Trail into the Florida Highwaymen Museum.

HOME AWAY FROM HOME

Why do Lake Worth Beach and Lantana have the largest Finnish population in Florida?

Finnish immigration to America peaked in the early 1900s when an estimated 300,000 poured into the country through Ellis Island. Some stayed in New York while others headed to the Midwest where the climate mimicked their Native land. They worked as carpenters and cooks for wealthy families who had the means to head south for the winter and bring their servants with them. Palm Beach, already established as a Gilded Age vacation hub, was the destination. A taste of tropical weather convinced many Finns to stay. Lake Worth Beach and Lantana, both across the Intracoastal Waterway from the island, offered affordable living for the wage-earners. In 1948, the Finnish Tourist Club was built and became the center of

A TALE OF TWO CITIES

WHAT: A network of friends from the happiest country in the world

WHERE: The Finland House is at 301 W Central Blvd. in Lantana.

COST: Event prices vary.

PRO TIP: Renovations to the Finland House have included the modernization of the ballroom theater and the addition of a Finnish mainstay—the sauna.

West Central Boulevard in front of the Finland House is known as Finlandia Boulevard. Photo courtesy of Finland House

Obstacles make eukonkanto, or wife-carrying, competitive. Photo by Tom Johnson

activity and a second family for the immigrants. By 2000, more than 600,000 Finns were living in the United States, including nearly 26,000 in Florida and an estimated 15,000 in Lake Worth Beach and Lantana. While the numbers have dwindled a bit—there are 12,000 or so Finns in the area today—the demographic is higher than anywhere else in the state. The Finnish Tourist Club, now called the Finland House, operates as a social organization with a full calendar of events aimed at maintaining interest in Finnish culture among the next generation.

The Midnight Sun Festival takes place every year at Lake Worth Beach's Bryant Park in reverence of Finland's traditions, a highlight of which is eukonkanto, or wife-carrying.

WET AND WILD

What sport has made the West Palm Beach facility internationally known?

With five lakes, four slalom courses, one jump ramp, and a group of volunteers who maintain the clubhouse, the docks, and the judges' towers, Okeeheelee Park is an epicenter for waterskiing. Named for the Seminole word meaning "quiet waters," the park is anything but when professionals are cutting, spraying, and zigzagging their way through the wake. The Goode Water Ski National Championships, the largest waterskiing competition in the world, has staged 16 shows there since 1986, each drawing a field of 700 to 900 athletes. The Ski Club of the Palm Beaches organizes events all year long that highlight the best that waterskiing offers—tricks. Handle passes behind the back, toe skiing on one foot, catching air, flipping,

A fisheye-lens view of Okeeheelee Park shows its vast expanse. Photos courtesy of Ski Club of the Palm Beaches

---

Okeeheelee Park is a 1,700-acre amenity that also has a 27-hole golf course, nine miles of equestrian trails, a BMX track, and the dog-friendly Pooch Pines green space.

OKEEHEELEE PARK

WHAT: An aquatic playground

WHERE: 7715 Forest Hill Blvd., West Palm Beach

COST: Free to explore

PRO TIP: One of the lakes at Okeeheelee Park fronts the Florida Turnpike, causing a lot of rubber-necking when skiers are flying by.

A skier angles himself to create an impressive wall of water.

and spinning, all while planing across the surface, are a thrill to watch. One of the slalom courses is lighted for nighttime runs. The club, in partnership with Palm Beach County Parks & Recreation, designed the lakes in 1981. Their width, length, and depth are engineered specifically for waterskiing as are their wave-absorbing, sloped shorelines. Only American Water Ski Association–approved vessels with permits can be launched. All the action is governed by a 110-page rule book that emphasizes safety.

CAN-DO COMPANY

What makes the small sweet shop so mighty?

Every confection, cup of coffee, and piece of pastry prepared at the corner store in Jupiter has a story behind it. Most of the apprentice chocolatiers, baristas, and chefs who toil over the tasty products are autistic. The adult son of the Chocolate Spectrum's founder is one of them. When Valerie Herskowitz, a speech pathologist, began teaching Blake how to mold candy, it gave him the joy of independence and an escape from the diagnosis he has dealt with since age 2. The noticeable transformation of her loved one led to the opening in 2016 of the nonprofit social enterprise. Its mission is changing the lives of those with developmental disabilities, and its success can be seen in the more than 100 trainees who have gained meaningful skills in a safe and sanitary setting where they interact with peers. The Chocolate Spectrum hires some of the trainees to run the café and the retail operation; three have been there since day one. Customers who purchase hand-dipped pretzels, old-fashioned fudge, trendy Dubai chocolate,

THE CHOCOLATE SPECTRUM

WHAT: A family-owned operation with a purpose

WHERE: 6725 W Indiantown Rd., Jupiter

COST: Prices vary.

PRO TIP: The Chocolate Spectrum accepts online orders and ships everywhere in the United States year-round.

Valerie Herskowitz's other son, Hunter, Blake's older brother, serves as a behavioral analyst and a teaching strategist for the Chocolate Spectrum's apprentices.

Above: *The Chocolate Spectrum team boxes goodies. Photo by Valerie Herskowitz*

Left: *The Chocolate Spectrum is open from 10 a.m. to 5 p.m. Mondays through Fridays and from 11 a.m. to 3 p.m. Saturdays. Photo by Lynda Pepper*

or truffles in flavors ranging from crème brûlée to lime support the cause as all proceeds go toward funding the program. Donations to the National Autism Registry also pay for the vocational initiative.

A DEAL GONE WRONG

Where did the creator of Mickey Mouse originally intend to build the theme park?

A few words and a quick handshake between Walt Disney, the pioneer of animation, and John D. MacArthur, the insurance salesman-turned-real-estate developer, christened 320 acres in Palm Beach Gardens as the location of a Florida version of Disneyland. Disneyland opened in 1955 on a razed orange grove in Anaheim, California., and by 1959, plans were in the works for another attraction in the Sunshine State. Disney World was to be built along the turnpike near PGA Boulevard, where the golf courses, resort, and spa of PGA National are today. Negotiations were kept under wraps for one year. By the time word had spread about the agreement and all that it implied, things had gone south. During a meeting in a penthouse suite at Palm Beach Towers, Roy Disney, Walt Disney's brother and business manager, upped the ante by demanding far more than 320 acres. The act of greed infuriated MacArthur, who stood up, excused himself from the room, and said on his way to the

DISNEY WORLD

WHAT: The room where it happened

WHERE: Palm Beach Towers is at 44 Cocoanut Row.

COST: Now a private condominium complex, the site is free to explore.

PRO TIP: The Magic Kingdom is an approximate 160 miles from PGA National and is less than a two-and-a-half-hour drive.

Disney World occupies 27,000 acres in the center of the state and, if placed on top of Palm Beach Gardens, would fill almost all of the city's 37,000 acres.

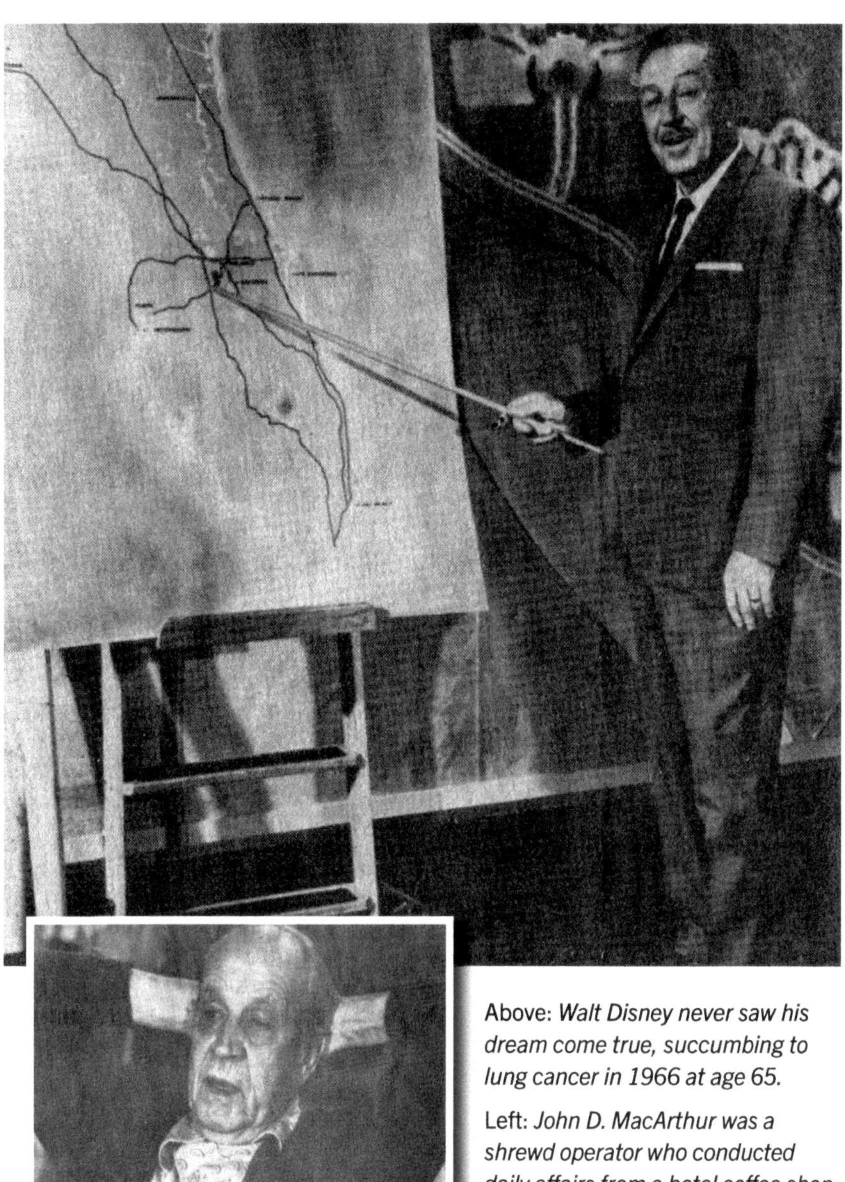

Above: *Walt Disney never saw his dream come true, succumbing to lung cancer in 1966 at age 65.*

Left: *John D. MacArthur was a shrewd operator who conducted daily affairs from a hotel coffee shop. Photos courtesy of Palm Beach Gardens Historical Society*

door, "I have to get the hell out of here or I'll hit that goddamn beagle right in the nose." In 1965, the Disney brothers announced plans to build the happiest place on earth in Orlando, and in 1971, Disney World debuted.

GOLDEN TICKET

Where is the 3,000-square-foot world of pure imagination?

Hundreds of flavors, shapes, and sizes of sugary goodness overflow from bins, and a selection of seriously scrumptious chocolate fills the shelves at the Bulk Candy Store in West Palm Beach. Everyone who enters the purple-and-yellow building—it has an enormous lollipop sticking out of the roadside sign—turns into a kid again. The retail space bursts with kaleidoscopic colors, and a delectable aroma fills the air. Aficionados in search of rare goodies such as Boston Baked Beans (candy-coated peanuts) or Dad's Old Fashioned Root Beer (hard candy that looks like barrels) will find them in stock. Owners Brian and Ken Shenkman, who opened the business in 1992, specialize in retro brands. The store carries international candy like Bananko bars (fluffy banana-marshmallow centers enveloped in European chocolate) and Swedish Fish (squishy red gummies) in addition to viral candy like liquid lollipops (sweet-and-sour goo in a squeezable tube). Peanut-butter cups the size of a

BULK CANDY STORE

WHAT: Sugar and spice and everything nice

WHERE: 235 N Jog Rd., West Palm Beach

COST: The store is free to visit. Tour prices vary.

PRO TIP: The Bulk Candy Store sells subscription boxes including a Popcorn Flavor of the Month surprise and a Sweets & Snacks package.

One of the more nostalgic displays on the Bulk Candy Store tour is a shadow box filled with movie props from 1971's *Willy Wonka & the Chocolate Factory.*

The Bulk Candy Store has been described as a paradise for candy lovers. Photo courtesy of Bulk Candy Store

pizza and 14-inch Pixy Stix in cherry, grape, and orange also are available. Tours of the facility explain the history of candy, candy making, and candy marketing and encompass six rooms decorated with a larger-than-life Pez dispenser, 100-year-old candy boxes, and other memorabilia. The 40-minute exploration comes with free samples and discounts on purchases.

GRASS ROOTS

How has Boca Raton's oldest neighborhood survived?

The grit of the Browns, the Clarks, and the Fountains along with the Goddards, the Wrights, and the other families who have inhabited a three-block section of Boca Raton since 1915 helped preserve its history. One of the few black communities in South Florida east of Dixie Highway, Pearl City has been a darling of developers for decades. "They have tried their darndest to get us out of here," Lois Dolphus Martin told the Boca Raton Historical Society in an interview leading up to the Pearl City Centennial Celebration. Idella Dolphus Glades also was interviewed, saying, "I don't care how much money they give me, I wouldn't sell it." They are not the only ones who thwarted local land barons. Many descendants of the first purchasers have rejected valuable offers, instead opting to stay put. Residents' voices ultimately were heard when Pearl City was put on the National Register of Historic Places in 2023. Originally established for farmworkers who

PEARL CITY

WHAT: An ungentrified slice of African American life

WHERE: Northeast 10th (Sapphire), 11th (Pearl), and 12th (Ruby) Sts.

COST: Free to explore

PRO TIP: A nonprofit called D.I.S.C. (Developing Interracial Social Change) of Pearl City was formed to enhance the quality of life in the little hamlet.

Pearl City's two churches, Macedonia A.M.E. on Northeast 11th (Pearl) Street and Ebenezer Missionary Baptist on Northeast 12th (Ruby) Street, still welcome worshippers to Sunday-morning services.

The Boca Raton City Council designated Pearl City a historic district in 2002. Photo courtesy of Boca Raton Historical Society

had been walking five-plus miles from Deerfield Beach to get to their fields, the property was to be governed "exclusively by colored people," an old newspaper advertisement stated. The early owners lived on Pearl, Ruby, and Sapphire Streets—they have been renamed to numbered streets—and opened a school, two churches, and small businesses during segregation.

SHINY AND SPIFFY

When did the antique fire engine roll out on its last call?

The 1925 American LaFrance that served Boca Raton for 40 years fought her final blaze in 1967. By that time, the Type 75 Triple Combination was showing her age. Unable to perform like the technically advanced newer trucks, Fire Engine No. 1, affectionately known as Old Betsy, was grounded. The doorless, windowless vehicle with steering on the right was cherished from day one. She was the town's only apparatus until 1946 yet assisted other municipalities during emergencies. When a hurricane knocked the water system offline at a Hollywood hotel, she pumped 750 gallons per minute for 100 consecutive hours. When she came to save the day in a smoldering Boca Raton neighborhood, one of the residents wrote a song about her. "The engine in charge of

OLD BETSY

WHAT: A retired responder vehicle with an "English hand"

WHERE: 100 S Ocean Blvd., Boca Raton

COST: Free to view

PRO TIP: To see Old Betsy, ring the doorbell at the fire station and ask someone on shift for a tour.

Above: *Old Betsy was listed on the National Register of Historic Places in 2001. Photo by Thomas Wood*

Opposite: *The American LaFrance that would become Old Betsy was photographed at the factory after production. Photo courtesy of American LaFrance*

Big Chief Bender comes tearing along as fast as they could send her," the lyrics go, referring to the first fire chief, Guy Bender. The department considered selling Old Betsy in 1968, prompting the crew to organize a restoration effort so she would not end up in the junkyard. New tires, fresh paint, and other touches throughout the decades eventually led to a complete overhaul in 1993. Today, the bright-red beauty looks like she did in 1925 and is safe and sound in an air-conditioned bay at Fire Station 3.

Old Betsy is 20 feet long, six feet wide, nine feet tall, has a 156-inch wheelbase, and weighs more than 9,000 pounds.

GREEN SPACE GALORE

Where is the largest facility of its kind in the world?

Halfway between the Palm Beach Zoo & Conservation Society and Trump International Golf Club, one dozen lush lawns blanket four scenic acres at the National Croquet Center in West Palm Beach. Those serious about the sport travel from around the globe to strike and score on the perfectly manicured grass. The 10-acre center is regarded as the crown jewel of six-wicket croquet, a competitive version that is distinctly different from the nine-wicket recreational version. Six-wicket croquet requires precision, skill, and strategy. Sturdy square wickets one-eighth of an inch wider than the ball replace flimsy wire hoops. One stake is used instead of two. The mallets are higher quality and often custom made. Those on the court must wear white. Despite its intensity, six-wicket croquet has experienced a recent revival and has come a long way since its origins in 13th-century France. The National Croquet Center serves as the home of the United States Croquet Association, established

THE NATIONAL CROQUET CENTER

WHAT: A timeless game that goes beyond the backyard

WHERE: 700 Florida Mango Rd., West Palm Beach

COST: Members only

PRO TIP: Beginners can sign up for two free lessons in golf croquet, yet another version of play, given at 9:30 a.m. Saturdays.

The man responsible for the National Croquet Center, the late Charles P. Steuber, of Boca Raton, spent his personal fortune on purchasing the land and funding the construction.

Top: *The National Croquet Center's wide verandas have sweeping views.*

Bottom: *The clubhouse is 19,000 square feet of colonial architecture. Photos courtesy of the National Croquet Center*

in 1977, and the Croquet Foundation of America, established in 1979. Both charitable organizations have a mission to promote the development and growth of the tradition-turned-trend. The Key West–style clubhouse houses the National Croquet Museum and its assorted collection of artwork, equipment, oddities, and trophies as well as the Croquet Hall of Fame with 118 inductees and counting.

BRING ON THE BRASS

What pieces of memorabilia are showcased at the West Palm Beach exhibit?

Guy Lombardo's baton, necktie, and black-and-white wingtips tell a story from behind the glass. So do Russ Morgan's trombone and Arthur Godfrey's guitar. One can almost smell cigarette smoke on the monogrammed jacket from Sammy Kaye's band. The worn batter head of Buddy Rich's drum conjures up images of the hitman's "fastest hands in the world" pounding out a solo. The Sally Bennett Big Band Hall of Fame Museum and its wall-to-wall collection of keepsakes celebrates the unforgettable sound that made Americans hit the dance floor. One display case takes viewers back to the origins of big band—jazz—and describes how early 20th-century instrumentalists wheeled through the streets of New Orleans in decorated wagons and influenced future artists like Louis Armstrong. Another display case delves into the period of sweet music that arose after the stock-market crash of 1929, bringing soothing arrangements from Hal Kemp, Wayne King, and others to the forefront. "King

SALLY BENNETT BIG BAND HALL OF FAME MUSEUM

WHAT: An ode to the leaders and the sidemen

WHERE: 9067 Southern Blvd.

COST: Free to visit

PRO TIP: The Sally Bennett Big Band Hall of Fame Museum is open from 10 a.m. to 4 p.m. Thursdays and Fridays.

The Sally Bennett Big Band Hall of Fame Museum, located in Yesteryear Village at the South Florida Fairgrounds, is the only museum in the country dedicated to the genre.

Top: *Sally Bennett first opened the museum in 1975 in Cleveland, and after several moves it found a forever home in 2005 in West Palm Beach.*

Bottom: *A creative vignette welcomes visitors to the Sally Bennett Big Band Hall of Fame Museum.*

of Swing" Benny Goodman and his groundbreaking performance at the Palomar Ballroom in Los Angeles is recounted as are the World War II years when trombonist Glenn Miller's Army Air Force Band became a patriotic bright spot. Sally Bennett, the museum's founder, was a successful composer who dedicated her life to honoring the bygone era's heritage and history.

SOURCES

Awkward Crook
palmbeachpost.com/story/news/local/2020/03/31/post-time-whos-sloan-in-sloans-curve/112255508

e-governmentresearch.blogspot.com/2020/01/a1a-sloans-curve-and-hurricane-of-1947.html

sloan.org

pbcpao.gov

Daunting Drive
palmbeachpreservation.org/landmarksdiscovered

Hidden Headstone
ghostsofpalmbeach.com/blog/johnnie-brown-and-laddie-best-of-friend

atlasobscura.com/places/grave-of-johnnie-brown-the-human-monkey

www.history.com/topics/1920s/scopes-trial

thecolonypalmbeach.com

Pauper's Field
pbchistoryonline.org/page/hurricane-of

palmbeachculture.com/black-cultural-heritage-trail-central-palm-beach-county

Chancery Lane Meets East Atlantic Avenue
theblueanchorpub.com

britannica.com/biography/jack-the-ripper

Towering Timber
royalpoincianachapel.org

tripadvisor.com/attraction_review-g34530-d12994248-reviews-giant_kapok_tree-palm_beach_florida.html

Finder's Folly
bbts.org

palmbeachpost.com/story/lifestyle/family/2012/10/26/look-what-we-found-antiquing/7602565007

palmbeach.floridaweekly.com/articles/collectors-corner-163

education.pbchistory.org/pbc-people/volk-john-l

Symbolic Shrine
palmbeach.floridaweekly.com/articles/sea-inspired-stained-glass-installed-at-st-marks

stmarkspbg.org/shared/documents/capital%20campaign/peace%20chapel%20brochure.pdf

church.stmarkspbg.org/ministry/partnerships

coventrycathedral.org.uk

Brotherhood of Bikers
enforcersmc.com

Fearless Farmers
morikami.org

Fields of Dreams
johnnybench.com

miracleleaguepalmbeachcounty.com

miracleleague.com

Hot Property
byjoecapozzi.com/post/how-you-can-peek-inside-the-melbourne-home-where-jim-morrison-of-the-doors-lived-as-an-infant

realtor.com/realestateandhomes-detail/2100-vernon-pl_melbourne_fl_32901_m66384-67848?msockid=02a1577e44a76bb21dda422a45f16a69

bcpao.us

Dreamy Digs

palmbeachpost.com/story/entertainment/2024/02/11/photos-of-john-lennon-in-palm-beach-come-to-town-in-may-pang-exhibit/72398783007

realtor.com/news/celebrity-real-estate/john-lennon-and-yoko-ono-owned-palm-beach-mansion-on-the-market/?msockid=02a1577e44a76bb21dda422a45f16a69

pbcpao.gov

commons.wikimedia.org/wiki/File:Lennons_by_Jack_Mitchell.jpg

Woodstock South

palmbeachpost.com/story/sponsor-story/2017/11/20/when-rolling-stones-played-and-partied-in-north-palm-beach-county/2545689007

oldrockphoto.com

history.com/topics/1960s/woodstock#woodstock-performers

Floating Relic

thehoneyfitz.com

Wildman of the Loxahatchee

youtu.be/aG_H7jsyJLU

pbghistory.org/post/the-legend-of-trapper-nelson-what-brought-him-here-and-how-he-died

floridastateparks.org/parks-and-trails/jonathan-dickinson-state-park/history

jupiter.fl.us/documentcenter/view/26433/trapper-nelson-a-rememberance

Football Factory

bellegladechamber.com/lawrence-will-museum

pro-football-reference.com

palmbeachpost.com/story/sports/high-school/football/2023/11/02/museum/71408084007

Cotton Club of the South

palmbeachculture.com/black-cultural-heritage-trail-central-palm-beach-county

Noteworthy Grounds

palmbeachculture.com/black-cultural-heritage-trail-central-palm-beach-county

nekishadurrett.com/genius-loci/131m031gjusbkt9frlfams9ys99cqm

wpbequalitytaskforce.org/the-styx-and-early-west-palm-beach-late-19th-early-20-century

Once a Barrier, Now a Bridge

palmbeachculture.com/black-cultural-heritage-trail-central-palm-beach-county

Secluded Beauty

worth-avenue.com

rickrosepalmbeach.com

Grande Dame

saturdayeveningpost.com/2023/11/marjorie-merriweather-post-the-philanthropic-heiress-who-built-mar-a-lago

newyorkalmanack.com/2025/01/architecture-of-joseph-urban-mar-a-lago-versus-new-school

thefamouspeople.com/profiles/marjorie-merriweather-post-31074.php

commons.wikimedia.org/wiki/File:Mar-a-Lago,_Palm_Beach._FL,_US.jpg

Art History

portraitsbydali.com

palmbeachpost.com/story/entertainment/local/2013/08/18/dali-s-grand-excess/6814006007

pbcpao.gov

onessimofineart.com/artist/salvador-dali

Talk of the Town

olmsted.org

pbchistoryonline.org/page/kelsey-city-lake-park

lakeparkflorida.gov

Storied Seafarer

palmbeach.floridaweekly.com/pageview/viewer/2016-05-26

Cacophony of Colors

lillypulitzer.com

Pink Paradise

thecolonypalmbeach.com

Portal to the Past

palmbeachcivic.org/once-secret-jfk-bunker-historic-coast-guard-buildings-in-line-for-repairs-reopening-as-county-park

westpalmbeach.com/jfks-doomsday-bunker-on-peanut-island

smithsonianmag.com/history/inside-jfks-secret-doomsday-bunker-180981574

pbcgov.com/pubInf/agenda/20250107/3m8d.pdf

flickr.com/photos/volk/3881006187

Hunting Grounds

antiquerowwpb.com

pbchistory.org

Digging Up the Past

palmbeachpast.org/2021/07/going-postal-1920s-style-the-strange-case-of-lena-clarke

historicalcrimedetective.com/the-murdering-postal-woman-lena-clarke-1921

Legend of the Seas

westpalmbeach.com/the-providencia-the-ship-that-named-palm-beach-and-west-palm-beach

findagrave.com

palmbeachpost.com/story/business/2012/03/27/palm-beach-county-s-oldest/7595399007

thepalmbeaches.com/providencia-award

Only in Nature

africafreak.com/sausage-tree

wildcraftia.com/plant/sausage-tree

beyondforest.org/post/the-sausage-tree-kigelia-africana

fourarts.org

gardenclubpalmbeach.com

Palace on Wheels

flaglermuseum.us

Entertainment Enclave

glazerhall.org

palmbeachcivic.org

palmbeachillustrated.com/raising-the-curtain-at-royal-poinciana-playhouse

loc.gov/pictures/resource/gsc.5a29969

loc.gov/pictures/resource/gsc.5a26236

Seaside Splendor

thebreakers.com

gallerieaccademia.it

Tasty Waves

tripstoexplore.com/best-beaches-for-surfing-florida

deepswell.com/surf-guide/US/South-Florida/Reef-Road/1204

More Than a Dot on the Map

palmbeachshoresfl.us

palmbeachpost.com/story/weather/2021/02/19/palm-beach-sand-transfer-plant-busted/6769329002

Power Couple

matrix.com/professional/our-history

findagrave.com

galeriemagazine.com/sydell-miller-peter-marino-la-reverie-christies

pbcpao.gov

Artist Extraordinaire

inflorida.com/news/jason-newsted-the-past-is-on-the-wall/509

thepalmbeaches.com/blog/10-best-murals-palm-beaches

palmbeach.floridaweekly.com/articles/back-to-his-roots

Back to Basics

palmbeachpreservation.org/education/little-red-schoolhouse

The Little Engine That Could

juno-beach.fl.us/history

jupiter.fl.us/documentcenter/view/321/the-celestial-rail-road

loc.gov/item/2016797329

Salty Piece of Land

palmbeachshoresfl.us

education.pbchistory.org/land-boom-bust/private-clubs

palmbeachpost.com/story/news/2013/01/24/blue-heron-bridge-third-to/7558689007

commons.wikimedia.org/wiki/File:Paris_Singer_of_Palm_Beach.jpg

commons.wikimedia.org/wiki/File:Singer_Model_27_1910_07.jpg

Leaky Teepee

palmbeachpost.com/story/entertainment/local/2018/08/30/happy-birthday-leaky-teepee-west/6940085007

palmbeachpost.com/story/entertainment/local/2017/08/16/elvis-presley-27-songs-he/7520893007

Take Me Out to the Ball Game

pbchistoryonline.org/page/baseball

pbchistoryonline.org/page/spring-training

baseballhall.org/hall-of-famers/mack-connie

deadballbaseball.com/2018/03/west-palm-beach-spring-training-history-connie-mack-field-and-municipal-stadium

britannica.com/biography/connie-mack

Formidable Fir

tampabay.com/environment/oh-florida-when-the-national-enquirer-produced-christmas-joy-not-political-scandal-20181220

palmbeachpost.com/story/lifestyle/2020/12/21/how-national-enquirers-christmas-tree-became-lantana-tradition/3963668001

boyntonhistory.org/christmas-magic-remembering-the-national-enquirer-christmas-tree parade.com/958326/walterscott/rockefeller-center-christmas-tree-facts

Metal Masterpiece

parkwestgallery.com/behind-the-artist-yaacov-agam

Fabled Fellowship

westpalmbeachfishingclub.org

Deal or No Deal

nbcnews.com/id/wbna20040247

abcnews.go.com/2020/story?id=2928554&page=1

thecoastalstar.com/profiles/blogs/briny-breezes-board-rejects-developer-s-502-5-million-offer-as-un

brinybreezes.us

Vivid Vegetation

gardenclubpalmbeach.com

esplanadepalmbeach.com

gsky.com/pro-wall

smilandscapearchitecture.com

Empty Graves

thecoastalstar.com/profiles/blogs/manalapan-60-years-on-chillingworth-murders-still-shocking

historicalcrimedetective.com/judge-chillingworth-1955

upi.com/archives/1982/07/05/the-ex-judge-who-plotted-and-directed-one-of-floridas/8862336908094

Altitudinous Experience

floridastateparks.org/learn/hobe-mountain

friendsofjdsp.org

Class Act

archive.clevelandartsprize.org/awardees/maltz.html

clevelandjewishnews.com/news/local_news/maltz-reflects-on-passion-for-broadcasting-in-new-book/article_e07fb4c0-f452-11eb-a083-9791935f931a.html

spymuseum.org

jupitertheatre.org

Titan of Technology

bocahistory.org/ibm-boca-raton

ibm.com/history

workatbric.com

Bold Form

palmbeachpost.com/story/news/local/2017/10/04/the-tallest-piece-public-art/7524571007

americanart.si.edu

albertpaley.com

Handsome and Hirsute

Reynolds, Burt and Winokur, Jon. *But Enough About Me*. G. P. Putnam's Sons, New York, 2015.

pbsc.edu

floridamemory.com/items/show/5822

Making the Cut

floridahistoricgolftrail.com

palmbeachpost.com/story/news/crime/2018/07/16/cold-case-murder-who-killed/6952270007

It's Showtime!

lakeworthplayhouse.org

byjoecapozzi.com/post/ghost-story-lake-worth-playhouse-centennial-stirs-spirits-of-the-oakley-brothers

Fictitious Name

palmbeachpost.com/story/news/local/2016/06/23/apix-secret-phony-town-in/7061421007

palmbeachpost.com/story/news/local/2018/05/23/post-time-pratt-whitney-opened/6804773007

floridamemory.com/items/show/31535

floridamemory.com/items/show/31536

Larger Than Life

Reed, Nathaniel. *A Different Vision: The History of the Hobe Sound Company and the Jupiter Island Club*. Reed Publishing, Hobe Sound, 2010

nathanielpreed.blogspot.com/2018/07/obituary-of-nathaniel-p-reed.html

Casa Apava

newyorksocialdiary.com/palm-beach-social-history

palmbeachpreservation.org

loc.gov/pictures/item/fl0186.color.572049c/resource

Toes in the Sand

facts.usps.com/no-official-motto

postalmuseum.si.edu/exhibition/networking-a-nation/terrain

floridamemory.com/items/show/295232

hypoluxo.org/community

theadventuresofcharliepierce.com

Meds and Malts
greenspb.com

Hanging with the Kennedys
forbes.com/sites/guymartin/2020/06/24/epic-real-estate-moves-former-kennedy-palm-beach-compound-reportedly-sold-by-billionaire-jane-goldman-for-a-cool-70-million

sub-culture.org/locations/camelot

townandcountrymag.com/leisure/travel-guide/g9154387/camelot-west-palm-beach

commons.wikimedia.org/wiki/File:John_F._Kennedy,_White_House_photo_portrait,_looking_up.jpg

Killing Field
Rommel, Keith. *The Devil Tree*. Sunbury Press, Mechanicsburg, PA, 2015.

archive.tcpalm.com/news/former-martin-county-deputys-killing-spree-in-1970s-still-one-of-most-gruesome-murders-in-st-lucie-e-345577182.html

truecrimearchives.blog/gerard-schaefer-the-killer-cops-reign-of-terror

Lions and Tapirs and Blue-Tongued Skinks, Oh My!
lioncountrysafari.com

Brave and Broad-Chested
jakovlje.com/stjepan-sipek-tarzan-iz-naseg-trnaca

imdb.com

erbzine.com/mag27/2772.html

Wow Factor
nature.org

beachbucketfoundation.org

inaturalist.org

Submerged Scenery
discover.pbc.gov/parks/locations/phil-foster.aspx

palmbeachpost.com/story/sponsor-story/2019/03/19/phil-foster-park-still-growing-after-all-these-years/5673792007

Fermenting and Fleecing
munyonspawpaw.com

sun-sentinel.com/2019/02/22/before-burning-down-this-island-resort-promised-cure-all-elixir-and-a-fountain-of-youth-it-was-one-of-floridas-earliest-swindles

macarthurbeach.org

digitalcommons.usf.edu/dunn_postcards/1137

Belly Up
ralphsstandupbar.com

jupiter.fl.us/documentcenter/view/303/jupiter-fire-department

jupiter.fl.us/documentcenter/view/1002/damon

Crucial Watershed
rivers.gov

loxahatcheeriver.org

Wise Guy
britannica.com/biography/al-capone

jupiter.fl.us/documentcenter/view/2034/prohibition_in_jupiter

palmbeachpost.com/story/news/history/2021/03/25/post-time-jupiter-farm-grew-tomatoes-before-capone-and-reynolds-bought-property/3610225001

miami-history.com/p/al-capone-in-miami-part-1-of-4

commons.wikimedia.org/wiki/File:Al_Capone_in_Florida.jpg

commons.wikimedia.org/wiki/File:Red_Bandit_Jacket.jpg

Living Archive
discover.pbc.gov/parks

trailoffloridasindianheritage.org/loxahatchee-river-park

loxahatcheebattlefield.com

Making a Splash
surfingfloridamuseum.org

Road Warriors
originalfloridahalloffame
highwaymen.org
backusmuseum.org
cityoffortpierce.com

Home Away from Home
thecoastalstar.com/profiles/blogs/finnish-centennial-independence-celebration-puts-nation-s-long-he
finlandhouseflorida.wpcomstaging.com
midnightsunfest.org

Wet and Wild
okeeski.com
discover.pbc.gov/parks

Can-Do Company
thechocolatespectrum.com

A Deal Gone Wrong
palmbeachpost.com/story/lifestyle/2015/12/10/how-old-man-macarthur-bullied/7295999007
palmbeachpost.com/story/news/2021/10/15/disney-world-could-have-been-built-palm-beach-gardens/8467770002

Golden Ticket
bulkcandystore.com

Grass Roots
bocahistory.org/pearl-city
thecoastalstar.com/profiles/blogs/boca-raton-pearl-city-clears-state-hurdle-for-national-register-r
discofpearlcity.org

Shiny and Spiffy
myboca.us
justacarguy.blogspot.com/2018/12/old-betsy-1925-american-lafrance-type.html

Green Space Galore
croquetnational.com
croquetworld.com/people/steuberobit.asp

Bring on the Brass
bigbandlibrary.com/specialcollectionsandarchivessally
bennettbigbandhalloffame.html
legacy.com/us/obituaries/sandiegouniontribune/name/sally-bennett-obituary?id=37369276

INDEX